The GRANDPA'S Manual

David Sutton, D-Min

and

I. Blake McKinley, DDS

ISBN 978-1-0980-9724-0 (paperback)
ISBN 978-1-0980-9725-7 (digital)

Christian Faith Publishing, Inc.
832 Park Avenue
Meadville, PA 16335
www.christianfaithpublishing.com

Printed in the United States of America

DEDICATIONS

This book is dedicated to my grandchildren, all twelve of them. It has always been my pleasure to see these grandchildren grow and face the challenges of life. They have, without exception, honored their family. Each one has especially brought joy to their parents and grandparents.

There have been bumps in their journeys through life, but with each bump, they have learned the lessons of God. I am most pleased with their accomplishments. As the younger ones continue to mature, they see the pathways in life that have been chiseled out by their older siblings. Their big brothers and sisters have distinguished themselves. I am confident the younger ones will follow the examples set before them and all of my grandchildren will continue to be challenged.

—I. Blake McKinley, DDS

I dedicate this book to my wife, Vickie, who has been my best critic. During our half century together, she has been my confidant and best friend. She has forever challenged me to embrace my passion for writing. As God blessed us with grandchildren, it became clear to me that Vickie is one of the best grandmothers I have ever seen. After hundreds of interviews and hours of research and reading, it was easy to come to this conclusion. As she demonstrated by example her patience, skills, and love for all of our grandkids, the lightbulb brightened in both our minds to seriously consider encouraging grandpas.

Vickie unselfishly encourages grandpas and grandmas to make a priority of establishing and maintaining a solid relationship with their grandkids. Her attention to details has sharpened the importance of this book. In every way, it would not have been written without her support and encouragement.

—David Sutton, D-Min

CONTENTS

PREFACE

Preface by Dave

One of my Grandpas and I hardly knew each other. It wasn't a bad thing because I was a little kid and didn't know better. Other kids at school had good relationships with their Grandpas, and it was special to them. My Grandpa sat in his old leather chair with a glass of goat's milk, chewing on a well-worn cigar. Most of the time, it seemed apparent he didn't even know we were standing right next to him, except when the baseball game or the news came on the radio. Then he would snap at us to be quiet. We didn't take offense. We just went in the other room.

For my mom's sake, I tried, as innocent as I was, to have a relationship with him like my friends. So Mom encouraged all of us to try and like Grandpa. We tagged along when he chopped the heads off chickens. We watched him milk the cow and the goat. He shot rabbits that invaded his garden. That was it. We barely talked to each other, but he was still our Grandpa. I even tried to stick to him like glue. I wanted to hang out with him despite those awful-smelling cigars. Nothing meaningful developed, and he died.

Then we met Slick, our Grandpa from the Ozark Mountains. They called him Slick probably because he had no hair. He and Grandma lived in a cabin in the woods and loved every one of their grandkids. It was exciting to

9

visit Slick because he always let us shoot his shotgun and showed us the best places in the country to hunt squirrels. We loved using his outhouse, and it was complete with a Sears-Roebuck catalog. We drew water from the well and used it up as fast as we could so we could return and pull up the bucket full of water again. We took our baths on Saturday nights in an old copper tub that looked much like a miniature horse trough. Grandma heated the water on the wood stove, and we took turns bathing right there in the kitchen.

Our relationship was fantastic. Slick rolled the rug back and grabbed his fiddle, usually on Saturday night after the baths, and we danced and jumped around. Charley brought his guitar with him, and Grandma played the jug while Uncle Pete plucked the Jew's harp. Dad and Slick sang, and the grandkids got to stay up past midnight.

We had some great times when we traveled to the Ozark Mountains to see Grandma and Slick.

My introduction to grandpahood crept up on me. Without warning, Grandma and I were presented a baby boy. Now I was a Grandpa, and I had no idea what to do.

I embraced my new role with dreams and fantasies. I dreamed of buying a new football for this future All-American wide receiver. Someday, we would ride motorcycles together in the woods. I thought about his first girlfriend. I already selected the instrument he would play in the band. He would wear nothing but Nike tennis shoes. My head was almost spinning with the thoughts. Then I realized my grandkid was only two weeks old.

Fifteen grandkids later, I decided to write a book about Grandpas. I could not find any evidence of somebody writing a book exclusively for Grandpas. So I seized the opportunity. Even with years of experience, I soon learned that there were other Grandpas who could consider me a rookie compared to their relationship and life with their grand-kids. As I interviewed other Grandpas, I learned that each one was quite different. The interviews consisted of a myriad of topics and dozens of stories. The more I searched for experienced Grandpas who were willing to share, the clearer it became to me that every Grandpa was as unique as a fingerprint.

Then I met Blake McKinley, a super Grandpa full of wisdom. He walked the walk and had a tremendous relationship with his grandkids. He and I agreed that we needed to write a book that encouraged Grandpas to establish a relationship with their grandkids. So *The Grandpa's Manual* was born. It is a book of stories filled with wisdom, humor, and encouragement. The book may test you. It can be challenging to others at times. It may raise your curiosity as to what kind of Grandpa you want to be. Hopefully, every story will enlighten you. It is not a how-to book. So any attempt for us to define your role or alter your relationship with your grandkids would be out of the question.

We would like everyone who picks it up and reads it to pause and say, "Hmm, I never thought of that!" Anyone can read *The Grandpa's Manual* and benefit from it. You do not need to be a Grandpa to enjoy it.

Some of the material in *The Grandpa's Manual* is packed with memories of our Grandpa's generation. They survived the Great Depression. They grew up before the Technological Age and did not experience drugs, free love, and the Sexual Revolution. What we learned from them are lessons of life that span all generations. The dress trends may differ, and they change from time to time. Many of our grandkids have multicolored hair and are pierced and tattooed. Hardly anybody is without a cell phone. Relationships take time, understanding, acceptance, and a great deal of effort.

age you to take on this challenge, knowing it may not be easy. But every step of the way will be worth it. Enjoy *The Grandpa's Manual.* We had a great time creating this gift just for you.

I. Blake McKinley, DDS

CONVERSATIONS WITH GRANDPA

Lay The Pig On The Table

One of our favorite sayings is "Lay the pig on the table." Using the phrase shows our Ozark background and farming childhood. This little gem of a phrase originated somewhere in the Ozark Mountains, we are told, and it means "to speak with no holds barred." The colloquial equivalent to the pig saying is "don't sugarcoat anything." It evolved as an act of genuine love, friendship, and concern for the other person. It is not a time to be hurtful or blameful. The discussion should deal with specific issues designed to help each other solve problems and steer away from potential situations that could create difficulties in relationships.

The saying was probably developed so that certain delicate subjects could be openly discussed. It creates a learning experience that sometimes results in agreeing to disagree. In the long run, things will be better as a result of approaching them with a kind and gracious attitude.

It is advisable, according to Grandpa, to ask permission before laying the pig on the table. In no way should you just start spouting off and being summarily rude or offensive. Asking permission puts both parties on the same page. Both are ready to hear things that may be unpleasant at first or lessons that may have never been learned. Either party may have been doing something damaging without realizing it. Or they have to receive a correction or rebuke. Asking permission projects an attitude of love. It eliminates a direction in the conversation that says, "I told you so!"

Grandpas are not required to have an opinion on everything. Sometimes being quiet is the best thing to do. But when speaking up is appropriate do so, it demonstrates that you genuinely care about your grandkids and are willing to do whatever you can to help and guide them.

Sometimes speaking up means you are protecting them.

Silence is not always golden. Sometimes you just have to lay the pig on the table.

Talk And Don't Lecture

Grandpa, do you remember when you were a parent and wanted to express upon your kids the idea of a life principle, like don't smoke or, before walking in the door, check your shoes if there is mud on them (then take them off). If your own kids did not say it out loud, they might have thought or communicated under their breath, "Here comes lecture number 34. Or lecture number 6." They had them numbered and could predict what was going to be said and how the hand motions and red face accompanied it.

In the long run, your lectures were more of a lesson for you instead of your kids. Dads lecture their kids when they do something wrong. Like most parents, lecturing is not very effective, and the kids know it. They secretly wish you would either change the script or take another approach.

Grandpa, you are no exception. Your grandkids are probably like most children when it comes to discipline and correction. Down deep, they want to be set straight. It's in their DNA. They were born that way. When they become resistant to correction, it is a result of not being taught properly. The end product of an untaught child is rebelliousness and, at worst, a child who memorizes your lectures and moves on without punishment.

The point is this: When we get involved in teaching our grandkids life principles, lectures are not the best way to get it done. Professors in college lecture. They have a captive audience who listens to them...or not. Students have to sit through the lectures. They pay money to be in class. It is the responsibility of the student to learn. The professor can make his spiel and walk away.

When Grandpa lectures, he can't walk away in like manner. And he probably does not have an office in which to talk it through. So the best way to correct, admonish, or reprove a grandkid is to throw the lecture out the window and order up a soft drink, ice cream, or fruit. And then talk.

Grandkids are not dumb. Instinctively, they know when they are caught or will be caught doing some forbidden thing. Some are slow learners. Some are not remorseful. Some may never learn. So Grandpa doesn't need to approach the council with a loud voice or a gruffness. The grandkids recognize that technique right off the bat. They have heard it before, not the contents of the speech but the method in which it is delivered.

So give this some thought. Being slow, kind, and gentle is better, period. Grandkids can actually become a little hesitant to spend time with anyone who lectures or yells at them. Talking it out is always more effective, and the learning curve increases.

Just a reminder, listening to your grandkids and having a genuine interest in what may be bothering them is always confidential. And because of the sensitivity, you should never usurp their parents. It wouldn't hurt to sidle up to your own kids and ask them how to handle the situation if it ever arises.

Embellishing

Grandma still reminds the grandkids, "Now remember, the older Grandpa gets, the better he used to be!"

"What does that mean, Grandma?"

"Well, it means that your Grandpa has done some very exciting things in his life that are all true. Each thing he did was so exciting. The more he tells the story, the more exciting it becomes. And the older Grandpa gets, the better he tells the stories."

Grandpa, it may have happened to you. You may have been telling a story to your grandkids, and gradually, the adrenaline starts pumping. Suddenly, the milk cows turn into charging bulls or the homemade go-karts become high-speed race cars. That fish may always be bigger than it really was. Or selling peanuts at the baseball park all of a sudden makes you part of the team. One of the privileges of being a grandpa is having permission to color the commentary a little bit.

So how does a Grandpa acquire the skill of embellishment?

Most of the time, it is a natural-born talent. It usually comes with age. Just the idea of making your grandkids laugh and marvel at the fact that their Grandpa did some exciting things is worth it. Turn an ordinary story into an adventure. Promote yourself to positions of grandeur. Laugh with them while polishing your storytelling technique.

One Grandpa tells the story of being a football player when he was young. Yessir, the other team was amazed at the mention of his name. He was an All-Conference linebacker. High school buddies talked about him. He must have been great. He certainly could spin a great tale.

The facts were all there: He played football in high school. He was third team Honorable Mention in the Class B League. The other team said he was such an ordinary linebacker it was amazing he even played the game. At high school class reunions, many of his buddies usually asked if he played more than one year. Of course, the story was embellished, and it made for a great time telling it to his grandkids. They ended up sharing stories about their football experiences.

Grandpa, you can mystify your grandkids with great stories and have a good time doing it, as long as all the facts are straight. Sometimes, it's just plain fun to joke around.

Being Alert

Grandpa, you are probably not a mind reader. But there are ways you can detect what your grandkids are thinking. Being alert to their body language, facial expressions, and timing can be clues as to why they initiated a conversation with you in the first place.

It may not be unusual for your grandkid to stop by just to talk. Many times, your grandkids will begin a conversation, and as you progress, you'll learn what they really wanted to talk about in the first place. Usually, it's the last thing they mention before they leave. Here's an example:

Grandpa was watching the football game when his grandkid walked in and said he came by for a cup of coffee and to just hang out. Grandpa poured his grandkid coffee and asked what was on his mind.

"I was thinking about that old car of yours. Is it fixable? I have a new app on my phone that lists parts for old cars. Are you interested?"

His grandkid never asked about the car before. He wiggled in his chair and would not look at Grandpa. *Suddenly, he wanted to know what it would take to fix it?* Grandpa thought to himself. He listed off parts they might need and told his grandkid about a plan he was developing to fix it, suspecting that that was not the real reason his grandkid came by to visit.

They talked about football and girls. They explored the idea of going on a safari. Both of them shared their political views. The afternoon went by fast.

It was time for his grandkid to go home for dinner. "Well, Grandpa, I'll see you later. By the way, what do you think about college? I'm thinking about going out of town to Harvey Mudd College. I like it, but so many people I talked to have never heard of it. What do you think?"

Without saying a word, Grandpa smiled at him. Both of them knew that was the real reason the grandkid came by originally. Then Grandpa said, "Let me think about it, but now, it's time to go home for dinner."

On his next visit, the grandkid began the conversation with "Well, what do you think?"

Being alert to all aspects of their conversation can act as a key to what's really on their minds. Good listening involves relaxing and focusing. They can pay great dividends when it comes to bonding with your grandkids.

Old Cars And Dreams

Grandpa, if you haven't already experienced it, spend some time with your fourteen- or fifteen-year-old grandkid and ask him about his favorite cars and the kind of car he wants when he can drive.

You might have done the same thing as your grandkids are doing when you were young, but your forgetter outweighed your rememberer. In other words, you probably wanted a car that was too expensive at the time and then tried to downsize your expectations and replace the luxury wheels for a lesser model.

Grandpa and his grandkid were spending some time together on Saturday, and the subject of cars came up. Grandpa innocently asked what kind of car his grandkid wanted. The answer was astounding.

Actually, he wanted to start with a DeLoren. Oh, it could be a used one because they were quite expensive. It was such a cool car, and an old broken-down one with multiple scratches on the stainless-steel body could sell for as little as $35,000.

Grandpa wanted to know how he was going to get that kind of money. His grandkid said he started a savings account and had put back almost $200. Then he admitted that the DeLoren was just his dream car. A Volkswagen bus was more in his range, and they were so neat and antique sweet. They didn't discuss price, but they did talk about availability. They were very rare.

At least they seemed to be making some progress. He was willing to downgrade to a cheaper set of wheels. He mentioned several other models and asked Grandpa's opinion on each one. They even stopped at a few car lots to see if they could find one. Perhaps a visit to the junkyard would have been more productive. Nevertheless, his dreams were real and, like most teenage dreamers who want to drive their own cars, one of two options could prevail. One, Mom and Dad could foot the bill on a mid-priced piece of transportation that would get him there and back. The downside of that was they got to choose the make and model. Two, saving up for the car had some merit, but it would involve getting a job and some discipline learning how to stash money back.

"What was your first car like, Grandpa?"

Considering the economy, the story of Grandpa's first car might seem unbelievable.

He told about his 1952 Ford. He paid forty dollars for it after towing it out of a farmer's field. He sold his bicycle to help pay for it. The engine worked great. The transmission needed some work. It slipped and sounded like an old car with the driver gunning the engine and going nowhere until the bands tightened, and suddenly, it moved and gained speed. On the drag strip, it could go from zero to sixty miles per hour in three minutes.

The crossover exhaust pipe had a hole in it, and the car sounded like a dragster running with straight pipe (no muffler). The interior needed cleaning, and the field mice were kicked out of their homes. It was purchased two months before a driver's license was issued, so he sat in it every night and roared the engine just to keep it warmed up. His dad said it was a waste of gas, and at twenty-five cents a gallon, that was a lot of money for a kid without a job.

So Grandpa continued the story. He drove it up to baseball practice illegally, hoping the shortstop's police officer dad was not there. He parked it on a hill above the baseball diamond just to show it off. It was about one hundred feet away from the backstop. In a dead run toward the plate, he was being cheered on because he was next up for batting practice. He fouled the first pitch over the backstop somewhere about one hundred feet toward his beloved Ford. It went directly into the windshield and stuck there. Grandpa just dropped his bat and went home in his car with a shattered windshield.

He sold it to the first baseman for ten dollars as is.

It's not the end of the story. Later, in his teen years, he owned a 1953 Packard (he ran up a guide wire on the way to a baseball game), a 1939 Chevrolet Century pickup (he blew the engine in a drag race with a 1948 Dodge), and a cherry-looking 1956 Buick Dynamic 88 (he drove into a field one night and ran over a fallen tree with a stump that had not been ground down).

His grandkid just looked at him.

"Don't you say a word, boy!" warned Grandpa. "At least not until we get a Coke."

Listen, Grandpa!

There comes a time when Grandpa may have to put some of his pride in his back pocket and make up his mind to just sit and listen to his grandkids.

Any honest, clear-thinking Grandpa may admit that the oldie-but-goodie guys don't have all the answers. They are vulnerable, and they make mistakes. But odds are that your wisdom and experience are much more useful than some other Grandpas. Not all times spent in a relationship with your grandkids needs to be learning experiences peppered with tons of wisdom and philosophy.

Sometimes, you just need to sit and listen and ask questions. Ask questions about what? The answer is, ask questions about everything.

For example, how do most of the kids at school spend their spare time? Why aren't more kids turning out for sports? What are girls thinking when they accept a date from a boy? What are the teachers teaching? And what do you think about that? If you could change anything in your school, what would it be?

Grandkids today are as different as the Grandpas who are trying to figure them out.

Yogi Berra, the great baseball player, once said, "I hear a lot by listening!" And how true it is. Not everything needs to be changed right away or be fixed by next week. Not everything will be agreed upon. And certainly, today is not like it was when you were growing up.

Here are a couple hints on how to listen to your grandkids: Somehow relate to them that it is okay to be different. Establish with them that you will agree to disagree (nothing personal). Sometimes advise tastes better when it ripens. In other words, timing is everything, and a quick answer or opinion isn't always necessary. It would be wise to think on it for a while. Moreover, not all things need to be fixed. If it is not illegal, immoral, or fattening, it may never need to be fixed. Fixing things is more successful when the fixer is asked to help, not when he jumps in and fixes it when it doesn't need to be fixed or your grandkids don't really want it fixed.

It is so important to understand what grandkids are doing and how they are thinking in these modern times. Being informed is like a wedge being used to pry open the door to their heart.

Perhaps the most effective element in a relationship based on love and concern is to let them be wrong for a while and then love them into being right.

The Military

"Grandpa, I was thinking about going in the Army, and it kind of scares me. I'm not into carrying a gun and marching everywhere. At least I don't want to make it a career. Is there anything else I can do or is there anything you did that was fun?"

"All five of the military branches offer training from cooking to computers to mortician to playing sports," Grandpa said.

At this point, it may help to make sure that you don't sound like a recruiter. In the same manner, you may consider not making it sound like so much fun that your grandkid can hardly wait to get to Basic Training. It's understandable that most young people want to know what it's like before they enlist. It only makes sense that they get the information from someone they trust.

One day, it will happen, Grandpa, and when it does, share the whole story.

Serving in the military is honorable. Not everyone shoots weapons and goes to war. But it is a fact that enlisting means you promise to defend the Constitution of the United States. Maybe that means going to war. But more importantly, young men and women who join an elite team of like-minded soldiers, sailors, airmen, Marines, and Coastguardsmen will be taken on a journey to the most unique job they ever had. Setting their Military Occupational Specialty (MOS) aside, they will wear the uniform of an American citizen who is willing to protect and fight for our freedoms.

So now Grandpa told a humorous story. It was about an adventurous life in the military. All in a single day, he said he laughed, almost cried, and jumped for joy. He told the story of driving for an hour to reach the troops who were conducting a field exercise. It was 111 degrees outside, and he and his partner were assigned to bring back photographs of the mock encounter with the "enemy" (who were other soldiers).

They took several pictures of the troops and were on their way back to Headquarters. The heat was sweltering as they drove through the outpost area, with the wind hitting them in the face like a blast furnace. Suddenly, they saw some cows in the field drinking from a mudhole. They decided a quick swim would be great. Nobody was around for miles, so they were not shy about taking off all their fatigues and running through the mud to sneak a quick dip. It was ugly mud. There were cow pies and frogs surrounding the edge of the "swimming pool." The cows just watched.

Both men ignored the hazards and dove in. It reminded them of the old swimming hole back home. Even in the hot sun, the water was cool. Who knew what was in that water? All of a sudden, one of the soldiers appeared to be attempting to walk on water as he exited the pool with great vigor. There they were, standing in the blazing hot sun in their birthday suits wondering what was in the water that attacked them. Quickly, they got dressed, climbed in the Jeep, and sped back to the barracks. They walked through the door of the billets smelling like a cow's watering hole.

"Where in the world have you guys been?" snapped the sergeant.

"Oh, on the way home we stopped and went frog gigging at an old watering hole," he fibbed.

"Never again." They laughed.

"Didn't you have the right bait?"

"No, but the frogs did!"

Then Grandpa said he often repeated the story and laughed as though he was telling it for the first time.

When they got back to work, they received a call from the Motor Pool. Everybody who had a Jeep had to paint it before going to evening chow. With a paintbrush, they were supposed to paint the vehicles olive drab with a white star on the hood. The two soldiers rushed over to the Motor Pool and checked out a gallon of paint. They quickly painted their Jeep and were ready for the white star.

The Motor Pool Sergeant came walking by and asked why the star wasn't painted on. The men said they were out of white paint.

"That doesn't matter," said the sergeant as he chewed the last of his cigar butt.

Both of the young soldiers said the response from the sergeant was so unbelievable they wanted to cry. The white paint arrived the next day.

Then came a great ending to a day that seemed to start out crazy: Weapon cleaning was canceled. That would make any soldier jump for joy.

Grandpa, it is to no avail for you to embellish war stories about the military. After training, soldiers pretty much settle in, and it becomes a job. Whether you served in the military or not, consider helping your grandkid progress as he or she takes strides to become a grown-up.

Speak Up! Or Where Did You Get Your Ideas?

Grandpa, your wisdom is a precious commodity. A silent Grandpa who knows he can gently interject good advice or opinion either creates confusion or adds to it. You can play a major role of being the family sage in many situations that call for experience, wit, and wisdom.

You should always be discerning in order to decide if offering your advice is appropriate. You should determine if your point of view will be accepted or rejected. Remaining silent may be the deciding factor in a serious discussion; however, if your opinion has been requested and if you have earned your position of respect in the family, you may need to speak up. Here is an opportunity for you to live by your own advice. "It's not what you say as much as how you say it."

Grandpa, your family may be looking to you for wisdom and advice. Speak your truth while caressing them with gentleness and kindness. Let them know you have walked that rocky road of life and you have glided down the smooth highways of joy and wisdom.

When you speak up, you are also making a statement that can be a contributing factor in the conversation. You may say, "This is my opinion and I believe it, but I could be wrong." By being willing to be incorrect, you can win the hearts of both your grandkids and the adults. Your willingness to learn while at the same time teaching is priceless.

If the time comes and your opinion is requested, seize the moment and speak up.

Speaking of communicating, where do you get your ideas, your wisdom, and your truth for your grandkids? Surely, you don't sit up all night thinking about them. Do ideas just come to you? When you plan a trip to the zoo, or organize a group to collect newspapers for charity, or set up a trip to all the bakeries in the county, is it a brainstorm or do you have a secret friend who is coaching you?

Every Grandpa must have a source of wisdom. Most of it comes from your journey through life. That journey may include getting fired a few times or winning the wrestling match at the County Fair. Maybe a road trip during spring break produced meeting a famous movie star. Experiences on that trip could have allowed you to stash some of the golden nuggets of wisdom to use when your grandkids came along. Most of your stories end with a lesson or a word of wisdom. Sometimes you do not have an answer, so you step up and admit it. Admitting you don't have all the answers is wisdom in itself.

Your grandkids learn to recognize fallibility and truthfulness when they see you come forth and confess your shortcomings.

Grandpa, you have the opportunity to encourage your grandkids to know that "age does not always bring wisdom, but the lack of age doesn't mean the absence of it." Finding sources for ideas that overflow with wisdom can be challenging. You can usually be at your best when you are just hanging out with your grandkids, talking, joking, and being a little crazy. Building a strong relationship takes work and imagination. It's always important to just let Grandpa be Grandpa and not some kind of guru.

Your best source of wisdom? Grandma, of course.

FUN WITH GRANDPA

Give Them A Laugh

Grandpa, once in a while, allow your grandkids to have a good laugh at your expense. Most of the time, they are laughing with and not at you. When you let them make you the center of their humor, you are allowing them to love you. They do it because they love you. This a good opportunity to cement your relationship with them. Sometimes by doing a few silly or crazy things, you set yourself up for some fun and humor.

For example, one Grandpa told his grandkids a story of one of his umpiring experiences. Prior to the start of a very large national tournament, he decided to promote the upcoming games by donning his school's umpire T-shirt and walking through a crowd of parents and players. He slowly ambled along with a white cane and sunglasses. He played the role to perfection. As he approached some parents, he asked where field 10 was. He explained he had a game there in the morning and wanted to check out the field conditions. One parent took him seriously at first and pointed in a direction. Grandpa simply touched his arm and whispered, "Don't point!"

They explained to him the layout of the fields, and he thanked them. As he walked away, he turned to the parent and said, "Nice red shirt."

They broke into laughter and pulled out their cameras. One parent hooked arms with him and actually wanted to lead him to the field. He reminded her that if it was too far to walk, he could always drive his car. It was a fun exhibition for all the umpires, players, and parents. The Umpire-in-Chief asked him to bring his cane and glasses and moderate the opening and welcoming of the initial umpire's meeting. His subject was "being at the correct angle in making close calls."

The whole thing was a little crazy, according to Grandpa, but it was fun. His grandkids made humorous remarks about him. Some were sarcastic but gentle, and everyone laughed.

Letting your grandkids have a laugh at your expense is good. You may even want to invite them to get crazy with you sometime.

Baking Bread With Grandpa

Grandpas usually like to tell stories about their grand-kids. But remember, some grandkids can spin some pretty good yarn themselves.

The report came through that this grandkid's Grandpa taught him how to bake bread. He soon discovered a major problem. So he tells the story.

Grandpa and I pulled out every pan in the house and lined up all the ingredients on the counter. At least we thought we had all the ingredients. Then Grandpa stood back, shook his head, and admitted he really did not know how to bake bread. He was nailed as he confessed. We uncovered some interesting things. When Grandpa said he knew how to bake bread, in actuality, he saw it done once, and it didn't look that difficult. He watched from the front window of the local bakery as one of the men appeared to be making bread.

One thing Grandpa did not take into account was a list of the ingredients needed to produce the dough. The baker made it from scratch.

So we decided to begin anyway. We took some flour. Grandpa said a half bowl looked like enough. It was going to be a small loaf. We added milk (not water) because we wanted it to taste better. Then Grandpa said we had to pull and tug at the dough to get the lumps out. So we divided the dough, put on gloves, and started to punch it. The salt and vanilla, baking soda and nuts, and sugar and yeast could be added later. We soon learned that kneading bread dough was an art, and it could be a real mess if you didn't know how to do it. We didn't know how to do it.

It was obvious we were not doing this the right way. So we took a break. Forget about the baker in the window. This was just enough of a challenge to drag out the cookbook.

We decided to try the country harvest bread. We had tasted it once at a little mountain café when we were hiking.

This delicacy called for molasses. We could not find any in the cupboard, so we decided to use Old Farmer's maple syrup. They probably tasted almost the same. When the recipe called for vegetable shortening, we were confused as to what vegetable it was referring to. So Grandpa found some stuff in a can that looked like lard, and we agreed that that would do just fine. Now the effort was intensified. We put all the ingredients in the bowl and waited for five minutes to let them all sink in to each other. Grandpa suddenly remembered he did not add the yeast. He ripped open two packages and sprinkled them in and waited about ten minutes. We didn't see anything happen, so we floured the countertop and started beating it. It was a little lumpy, but we could work that out.

The instructions said to place the dough in a warm place and let it sit for an hour. The warmest spot in the house was the furnace room, so we put it there. If one hour was good, two hours must be better. So we took a nap. When we awoke, we raced downstairs only to find enough dough in the furnace room and the adjacent bedroom to make several loaves. We knew we were short on bread pans, so we found a huge kettle, greased it with butter so as to make it taste better, and heated up the oven.

We just assumed again that more was better when it came to beating the dough to death, so we kneaded it vigorously. We gave it about twenty-five minutes to cook, removed it from the oven, and laid it on the table to cool.

We tried to slice it, but that didn't work. We used a makeshift chisel and tried to crack it open. That didn't work either, so we tossed it on the floor, and it cracked a little. We reached in the crust, took a small piece of dough, and tasted it. Without saying a word, we looked for something to wrap it in and headed for the dumpster.

We raced to the local bakery and bought a loaf of country harvest bread. Arriving back at home, we came in the side door by the kitchen and thought it would look good to leave our mess as it was. It appeared we tried really hard. Grandpa placed the bread on the stove thinking Grandma might at least be impressed by our efforts.

That didn't work either.

The Thrift Store

Being thrifty is a skill and some people even call it a sport.

Some Grandpas use the old-fashioned term *junking* instead of Thrift Store shopping. The difference in terms can be found in the quality of the goods. Junk is just throw-away stuff. You know one man's junk is another man's treasure. But a thrift store carries high-quality junk. And the adventure of wading through a Secondhand Store with your grandkids can be fun and delightful. It also can be a learning experience for you. You can close the generation gap by learning what your grandkids know and don't know about things of the past.

A trip to the thrift store with your grandkids for the first time could certainly open their eyes to the past and learn how Grandpa lived during the olden days.

Those young junkers will come home with stories you can't make up. Like the time they came across a cassette player. They had no idea what it was. Try explaining it to a ten-year-old. He shook it, rubbed it, pushed buttons, and still couldn't figure it out. He finally discovered that it needed a cassette. The owner came over and demonstrated. The light finally came on as Fats Domino wailed out "Blueberry Hill."

Then the young explorers came across one of those old milk cans. The explanation given by the owner was great. But the grandkids walked away scratching their heads wondering how you got the can under the cow to get the milk.

There isn't a thrift store in existence that does not have a necktie section. The grandkids knew what neckties were, but they marveled as history was opened up before their very eyes. Wide ones, thin ones, sexy ones, dull ones, and novel ones. Each had a story about the generation in which they were fashionable. They quickly decided that none of them would ever been seen in a Norman Rockwell tie. They are nice and probably will never go out of style. But original Jerry Garcia ties are much cooler, if you can find one.

Finally, they discovered a homemade ice cream maker. The announcement was made that a dollar bill would go to the first one who could figure out what it was.

"You mean you made your own ice cream, Grandpa?"

"You bet we did," he said proudly.

They played with it for a while as each of them took a turn cranking the handle. Then they questioned how sitting there turning a crank could be much fun. Imagine gathering the whole family in the kitchen watching people take turns cranking the handle. Even fresh popcorn couldn't add glamour to that party.

The pinnacle came when they arrived at home. The grandkids had some great stories, and they challenged Grandpa to forget all that old junk. They explained how they wanted him to be up-to-date. They said, "Loosen up a little. How can you still wear that those old-style clothes?"

The next time they met for an adventure, Grandpa was wearing acid-washed jeans with holes in them and red tennis shoes. They were impressed. Nobody ever suspected that he didn't buy the acid-faded jeans with holes in them for $58 at JCPenney. He also just kept walking past the shoe store that sold $100 red Converse sneakers. So there they were, standing in the mall, a couple of proud teenagers with their updated Grandpa. And he was dressed to the nines for less than ten bucks.

Washing The Dog

There are some Grandpas that have the skill of getting the job done no matter what. "Whatever it takes" is their motto.

Quite often, Grandma doesn't sugarcoat anything and usually proclaims, "If there is a way to mess something up, Grandpa will figure it out!"

Take giving the dog a bath, for instance. Most dirty dogs who need cleaning in the worst way will either be taken to the local Doggie Wash, or they will fight like an Australian dingo to keep from being thrown in the bathtub upstairs. If Grandpa has even an ounce of practicality in him, neither method will work. This Grandpa takes the dog in the shower with him. Yep, the dog takes a shower.

Now, we pretty much know that not all dogs like the water. Some of them do. But make sure you read the situation and assure yourself that your dog is water-soluble before putting him in the shower. If your dog does not like the way you scrub him, then expect a battle to ensue and be prepared to allow Grandma to remodel the shower stall.

The adventure can be quite easy. First, the dog must be a water spaniel or related to one. Second, human shampoo is acceptable as long as you don't announce it to Grandma. And a little conditioner couldn't hurt either. Doggie shampoo is overrated. Third, never allow your grandkid to speak during the procedure. The dog will go bonkers if he hears the kid cheering for you or him. Disaster could result. Fourth, swear your grandkid to secrecy. Not a word needs to be said about what towel was used or how many towels it took to dry Fido. What residue was left on the shower floor does not need to be announced. And nothing ever needs to be said about Grandpa's attire in the shower or the lack thereof. The grandkids need to be indoctrinated as to how sacred this ritual really is; the details of which should never be discussed.

The success of the project can be seen in a happy, clean dog that looks and feels great. But success can also be seen in a wink from Grandpa at the grandkids, indicating secret bonding as they both burst with pride. What a great way to spend the day with Grandpa. Is that cool or what?

A Day At Work With Grandpa

Take Your Kid to Work with You Day can backfire. Grandpa, do you have any knowledge where this idea came from? Have you ever taken your grandkid to work with you?

Perhaps the thinking for this special day came about to encourage kids to see what Dad did at work. For some kids whose dads were nuclear engineers, garbage collectors, doctors, or salesmen, for example, the concept may have seemed exciting and interesting. But their dads presented a good case for his kids to stay at home that day. Usually, the safety of the children was the primary reason.

So the grandkids introduced Take Your Grandkid to Work Day. The same concept applied, and the grandkids had an opportunity to be in the adult workforce just as they would have with their dads. Grandpa was most likely retired, and his "job" was volunteer work or light professional tasks. In this case, Grandpa was a minister and had been asked to perform a wedding. After checking with the bride and groom and asking for permission, he invited his grandkids to accompany him.

This was no ordinary wedding. It was in the backyard, and nobody took the time to mow the grass or clean up the area. With three dogs in that family, the yard could have used a little grooming.

The folding chairs were placed lopsided in front of the homemade altar, which was a long, bare utility table. The music was provided by the next-door neighbor who was touted as an excellent musician. She set up her boom box with a handful of CDs behind the tool shed. The bride provided extra speakers and a card table for her work space. The prelude was done to perfection. Eric Clapton and Cream played the original version of "Crossroads." The guests appeared to be loosening up as they danced but not before they dipped into the tub of beer and cracked a cold one. The music segued into a gentler song by Bette Midler, and the bride prepared to make her entrance. Her newly pressed cutoff jeans were accented with sequins. The colors of her shorts and tank top were coordinated. She carried a bouquet of freshly snipped yellow flowers from the front yard.

The bridegroom and his best man stood at the altar waiting for her arrival. They wore matching bowling shirts with bolo ties. The best man quickly extinguished his cigarette but not before the bridegroom sneaked a puff. Both men wore similar cutoff jeans and sandals with socks. The maid of honor preceded the bride down the makeshift aisle. Three white bath towels covered the uneven lawn, outlining the pathway.

The maid of honor wore a silk gown with a loose bodice, a fashionable hat, and elbow-length gloves. Her outfit was accented with spiked heels.

Grandpa cleared his throat and began. Suddenly, two of the dogs came rushing down the makeshift aisle, full of energy and willing to lick anyone. The bride dropped her flowers and started swearing like a sailor. She chased the dogs into the garage and tried to slam the door shut. The dogs avoided the door and escaped. This time, the bridegroom left the altar and grabbed them both by the neck and vividly described what kind of dogs they were. Grandpa just stood there.

The audience applauded, cheered, and took a break at the beer tub. This wedding was completely out of control. Grandpa approached his grandkids and invited them to wait in the car if they wanted to. They declined and said this was the coolest wedding they ever attended. Being a pastor was more fun than they had ever thought.

The ceremony continued into the dark hours. The beer was running low, and the groomsmen increased in number to six. The maid of honor went solo.

Grandpa was giving serious thought to leaving. He conferred with the couple, and they agreed that the ceremony was just grand. Grandpa somehow got everyone to stand at the dilapidated folding table, and he pronounced the couple husband and wife. Everyone kissed each other, and Grandpa agreed to meet them at noon the next day to sign the papers.

The trip home was a quiet one. Halfway there, the grandkids could not hold back any longer and busted out laughing. Grandpa joined them.

It was a struggle, but Grandpa finally proclaimed that a sign of maturity was to take control when nobody else was willing to.

Who would have ever thought going to work with Grandpa could be so interesting?

Crossword Puzzles

Grandkids need to be introduced to crossword puzzles at an early age, and Grandpa is the most likely candidate to get the job done.

Why Grandpa? Because he is a veteran at playing the word game, and he has the time. You may say it is part of his responsibility to help his grandkids experience every opportunity available to be educated. Anyway, it's really fun and challenging.

Grandpa reasons, "Who wouldn't welcome a chance to learn new words they probably will never use again in their lifetime?"

Part of the fun in working crossword puzzles is to know where to look up the answer. It's thrilling to see a newcomer reach for the *Crossword Dictionary* and get the word right. Siri is a great source. It gives the grandkids a sense of accomplishment knowing that they are becoming really smart. And they are smart if they learn how to look it up. Looking up the answer is a skill in itself.

Grandpa and Grandma appear to be quite intelligent in the eyes of their grandkids. After all, they have spent hours and hours working the puzzles. How many ordinary people know what a qat is? And who wouldn't get excited remembering it was Grandpa who introduced them to his first qajaq and told the story of earning sheqalim when times were tough.

The mystery of those little squares that Grandpa cannot wait to attack every morning can spark a fire of enthusiasm for the day. And Grandpa encourages his grandkids to share that time with him, honing the skill of conquering the puzzles.

With two sharpened pencils, he pours a cup of hot java, grabs the newspaper, and begins to cogitate.

What in the world is a zelkova? He pushes out his chair, takes a sip of coffee, and goes upstairs to ask Grandma.

Glossary

qat. An evergreen shrub.
qajaq. A kayak or one-man boat.
sheqalim. Same as a shekel.
zelkova. A Japanese tree.

SPENDING TIME WITH GRANDPA

Hanging Out With Grandpa

Grandpa, try to avoid letting age difference make you an old fogey.

Being the sage in the family is a noble title. The wisdom is certainly appreciated, and it is usually well received. But there comes a time when a Grandpa may benefit by taking the risk of being a kid just like his grandkids and having a real blast.

If you have never tried it, challenge them to a race in Go-Karts. Yes, that's right, Go-Karts. Those little racers can go speeds upward toward twenty-nine miles per hour on an indoor track. They are safe, and it's a real rush of adrenaline. At one go-kart track, the man who holds the local speed record at the indoor track is a ninety-two-year-old former dirt track racer, and nobody can beat him on the indoor track. You may even outrace your own grandkids and show them who is the boss. Have a great afternoon at the race track. Most tracks monitor each race and provide information about speeds, time, numbers of laps the driver led in the race, and much more.

Think about it. What's so bad about eating twelve different kinds of ice cream in one sitting? It'll probably spoil your dinner. But who wants to have dinner if you are bloated? One of the grandkids may even suggest a competitive way of emptying your stomach, like a challenge to drink a full soda pop in less than a minute. You may want to skip that one.

Can you ever imagine eating your way through the Farmer's Market? Find one that offers fresh everything, and take your time sampling everything. Make sure you have a story behind every entrée. Let the kids know it's okay to dress up their stories a little, and then offer a prize to the one who does the best job. It is essential not to skip a vegetable booth or a fruit stand or a roasted duck display. One Farmer's Market had fresh raw salmon, raw tuna, and unique delicacies, like baked fish eyes and frog legs. You wouldn't want to miss any of that.

It can be fun, hilarious, and inviting to spend an afternoon trying on clothes. Chances are, the store clerk will approve of it because an old, gray-haired guy with kids will take responsibility. Don't forget to take your camera and record the adventure. When you have root beer floats afterward, you can share stories about the clothes. Urge each grandkid to tell a story about why he chose those particular clothes.

The point of it all is to hang out with grandkids. Figure out what to do. It really doesn't matter as long as it's fun. Remember to make sure everything you do is legal, fattening, or utterly corny.

Spending Three Or Four Days With Grandpa

One of the best things a Grandpa can do for his grand-kids and himself is to invite them to stay with him and Grandma for three or four days.

This could be a very rewarding time and a great opportunity to bond or establish a relationship. It doesn't always need to be a minicamp for learning the principles of life. It can be fun and adventuresome.

Make sure you have something up your sleeve besides your elbow when the grandkids come over. Have an agenda of activities that could include doing a little bit of work, having a crazy time, exploring, and hanging out. Eliminate an opportunity for them to plug in their video games. Cell phones are an option.

One Grandpa was sharing about his adventures with his dog. His grandkid said, "Someday, I sure would like to have a dog, Grandpa."

"That's a great idea. Let's make sure your mom and dad will approve of it."

So they set out together to seek parental approval. Then started the bonding. Mom and Dad said okay, so the dog now needed a place to live. Pull out the hammer and nails and the saws and the trimming. Lay out the paper on the drawing board and draw up the plans together. Then got busy building.

Another Grandpa reported that his grandkids had a "jillion" questions about one particular subject. He admitted he didn't know everything about it and didn't have all the answers, but he had books waiting for them so they could look up the answers together. They spent hours reading the books and using the computer. The days came to an end, and the bond was tighter than ever before.

A great experience during the visit was hanging out a little bit with Grandma. She could just marvel at the opportunity to teach the grandkids how to make a cake or bake cookies. They could pick some raspberries together or make bread from scratch.

There are tons of things you could do. But the most important is the bonding. The grandkids will remember forever the time they spent three or four days with Grandpa and Grandma.

And Grandpa is likely to never forget.

Baseball Game With Grandpa

Not all Grandpas are able to throw a baseball around, shoot baskets, or demonstrate the skills of tackling, punting, or passing.

One substitute for the lack of skill or ability is to take your grandkids to a sporting event.

Amateur sports are not really games. They are disguised as methods of learning about life. Part of life is competitiveness. Granted, some people overreact to competition, and others may deny its value. Take for instance your favorite team. Everyone wants their favorite team to win, so they cheer them on. The competitiveness of one team attempting to beat their opponent is what usually encourages us to root and cheer.

Part of life is learning a skill. Being a good athlete never comes without practice and focus. A natural athlete is a person who is gifted with coordination and other skills needed to excel. But he or she goes nowhere without focus and practice.

And the list of examples goes on. But one of the greatest lessons in life that can be gleaned from sports is sharing a game with your grandkids. Take them out to the ball game. Go to a basketball game. See a hockey game or attend a wrestling match. It can be on any level so long as you have your grandkid with you.

For instance, what can be taught at a baseball game? Life is full of decisions that have consequences. The baserunner must decide if stealing a base is a good idea. He watches the catcher to see if he has a good arm while examining the moves of the pitcher. If the pitcher has a slow delivery, it may be an indication the baserunner can successfully steal a base. If the decision is wrong, he is out. If it is right, he advances or may score a run.

There are some skills you can pass on to your grandkids at a baseball game, like yelling at the umpire. That's quite a technique. You are not allowed to say anything personal about the umpire, for instance. It's just not nice, but some people think it's part of the game. It can be fun to yell at him from the stands and comment about his eyesight. Tell him he is missing a great game. Evaluate his strike zone.

The fun thing about being at a baseball game with your grandkids is eating and drinking. There are always boxes of Cracker Jacks and sunflower seeds along with overpriced soda, cold wieners, and soft ice cream. You buy them anyway and just scream and yell along with everyone else. Assure your grandkids you are an expert on the game because you played it.

Football and basketball games aren't much different. It's the company you keep. You can know little about the game, but high-fiving or jumping up and down in the bleachers can add to the fun. Everybody likes to see and hear a great tackle in football. And three-pointers in basketball always raise the roof. It's difficult to sit still when you and your grandkids are part of the crowd, screaming and yelling together while sharing handshakes with loyal fans around you. Grandpa, remember, there is value in watching sports with your grandkids. You don't even need to be a sports fan. Just you and your grandkids being there together is a great part of the game.

DIFFICULT CONVERSATIONS FOR GRANDPA

First Love

When your grandkid loses his first true love, his world can come tumbling down. What can he do, and where can he go? Grandpa may be first on the list for him to seek comfort and counsel.

Why? The answer is not all that complicated, but it does merit some explanation. Mom is out because she is a girl. Dad is out because he tends to make light of it. Brother will laugh, and well, forget sister. She may be his first love's friend, and then nothing will ever be sacred.

So you become the go-to man. Your grandkid can always trust you to keep quiet. You won't laugh at him or make fun. You hopefully will not tell him there are other fish in the sea. And most of the time, you have been in that situation at least once and can identify with a young boy who thinks he is probably the only kid in the world who has ever been dumped.

So what happened? In this case, your grandson and his girlfriend Pam were almost always together. When they separated, it was usually because he played football and she twirled her baton in the band. She went to every football game and practice when she was not with the band. After practice, he walked her home. What dedication. It was usually dark and was two miles out of his way. And after a sweaty football or wrestling or baseball practice, his loyalty could not be questioned. Then along came Sam, and suddenly, it was all over. He had a cooler bicycle, dressed better, and was in the band.

"Did she break your heart?" you asked.

"Yes, into 1,300 small pieces."

"Did it break her heart or even show signs of anything?"

"What heart? I thought she loved me too. We even talked it over and decided to get married but not right now. We are only twelve years old!"

That was a good call. It seemed as though there should have been two broken hearts. Without taking sides, you gently inquired about your grandkid's feelings toward her right now. That kid was so in love that an atomic blast could not have separated them. He still had feelings for her. Then with equal gentleness, ask what she thought about him. Just listen and let him cry and pound the pillow. The impression was that the relationship was seemingly lopsided.

They just sat there in the grandkid's fort for hours. It was so sad yet so typical for a junior high.

A variety of subjects came up. Some of them targeted the breakup. Others centered around the National Football League. As a diversion, Grandpa took the conversation to places unknown. But focus eventually came back to Pam. Even Grandpa's 1960s music by Del Shannon, Fats Domino, and The Supremes didn't penetrate the barrier. The poor guy lost his life's true love, and she dumped him for a guy with a fancier bicycle who could play both the clarinet and the drums.

Grandpa, sometimes in situations like this, a solution to the problem may not help at all. Obviously, the young boy and the girl are too young to be that involved. But puppy love is always real to the puppy. Your solution, if there is one, should be delivered with kindness and gentleness. Treat it as very serious and wait for nature to take its course. Show love for your grandkid even more and be sure to remember to let him bring it up next time and not you. They got married after he was in the Army and started a career. He remained single. She was a young widow. One day, twenty-five years later, they met at the local grocery store for the first time since junior high. And so it goes.

Death And Dying

Grandpa was sitting on the porch with his grandkid working on a Diet Pepsi with a wilted straw. They were just relaxing and casually asking each other questions. It was a game. It didn't matter what the question was; each one was received and answered with grace and honesty. They just laughed at some of the questions because they were borderline ridiculous, and some of them were downright silly. Then his grandkid asked, "Grandpa, what is it like to die?"

Grandpa nearly choked on his Diet Pepsi and probably used the cleanup time to think on the question. He wiggled back in the porch swing and made his answer quick and seemingly lighthearted.

"I really don't know because I have never died!"

He was hoping that his answer was satisfactory and that they would continue playing their game. It wasn't adequate, and both of them put on a serious face.

He admitted he wasn't a Bible scholar, but he went to Sunday School most of his life. He remembered that his Sunday School teacher had predicted that one day this might happen. He said when it did happen, the men in the class should give a straight answer and try not to sound religious. He even mentioned that too many details may scare the daylights out of their grandkids. The challenge was there, and Grandpa began.

"First, you know we all are going to die sometime. It is not an option, and that is just the way it is. We were made that way. If we didn't die then we might live to be a thousand years old. I wouldn't want to do that!"

His second point was direct. He told his grandkid that when we die, we go someplace. He winked and said, "We either go up or we go down. Do you know what I mean?" The grandkid got the picture.

Third, we need to understand that we are a spirit living in a body. So when we die, our spirit is the thing that goes somewhere, and our body is of no use to us. So it is either buried or cremated, burned up.

"What happens then, Grandpa?"

So he told about everybody getting a new body. He said he had no idea what it would look like. Some people guess we would have wings, sitting on a cloud and plucking on harps all day. They both giggled when Grandpa said he didn't even know how to play the harp.

The conversation lasted for about an hour, and his grandkid had more questions about heaven and the "other place." At first, Grandpa struggled as he opened another Diet Pepsi. That gave him some time to think.

"I really don't know a lot about that," he said honestly. "Let me think on it for a little while."

He concluded with the information his grandkid might have been seeking in the first place. He said he really didn't know about the actual dying part. But he guessed that it might be like going to sleep. When you woke up, you were in another place.

"Grandpa, I sure hope you are okay!"

Grandpa could sense what the boy was referring to, so he put his arm around him and gently squeezed. They were just there and hugged for a minute.

Then Grandpa said, "Son, I know I won't be around forever, but while I am here on earth, I promise to love you from your toes clear up to the sky every day. And you can count on it!"

Guns

It seems like packing a pistol is becoming a popular thing nowadays. Grandpa, do you carry a concealed weapon? You can be relatively sure that one day, your grandkids will ask that question, and he or she will want to know why or why not. What are you going to tell them?

Keeping with our Grandpa guidelines, be honest. Let's look at a couple of ways this subject may be expanded upon.

First, we have the right to bear arms, according to the United States Constitution. We have the right to defend ourselves and our family and property. That does not mean we can go around shooting people like they did in the Wild West. It means that nobody can threaten your life or harm you or your family. Also, this is so important that it is stressed at Gun Training and Safety courses before you strap on your pistol. In those gun safety courses, they teach you what "life-threatening" means and how you can deal with it. Other things include teaching gun safety and proper handling of a weapon. Never take on the responsibility of owning a gun until you take the training. Carrying a weapon can give an illusion of strength and control.

Now, if you do not carry a weapon, what can you say? Many people have said that carrying a gun gives them a sense of "false security" whereby it is easy to adopt an attitude of being available to help when somebody else is being threatened, like in a robbery or mugging. By "false security," we mean getting involved in a situation that may cause danger to you because you have a weapon. In those cases, sometimes it's better to hide or run. Why else would you not carry a gun? There are several other reasons, like it's too expensive, it can be dangerous with small kids in the house, or it can just be plain not liking guns. Whatever the reason, be up front with your grandkids and get their input. This will be a great time for you to learn a thing or two about what they think.

The bottom line is this: We live in the greatest county in the world, and we have the freedom to protect ourselves. Whether it's taking a course in karate or carrying a gun, we have that right to choose.

Spiritual Things

Grandpa, there will be a time when your grandkids will come to you and ask about things that may be difficult to explain. They will expect an answer. Don't be taken by surprise. Be prepared.

Of course, we are talking about spiritual things. Church stuff. The Bible. God.

You do not have to be a theologian or minister to receive their inquiries. But you should be honest.

There are at least two ways to approach this subject. Here are examples of each one.

If you do not lean toward God things, say so. Your grandkid would much rather hear you say what you believe and where you are than to struggle through you trying to fake it. Be assured that this is not as scary or difficult as you think. In this first method of laying out an honest explanation begins at the beginning.

Start with God. He made everything. And then move to Adam and Eve. They broke the rules, so they had to pay the consequences. Then tell what you know about good and bad. Explain why evil is bad and why good is good. You will find that this can be a very comfortable approach. But be ready for some genuine questions. You may want to respond with "I don't know" or "I am not sure." That may be sufficient.

Or you may want to answer a question with a question. "What do you know about this? You tell me, and maybe Grandpa and you can learn together."

The second approach is similar. Always be honest, of course. And tell what you know. But the second approach uses a little more information.

Begin by telling your grandkids about your experience with God and the church. One Grandpa shared about himself in order to make it more personal.

He said, "Once there was something wrong in my life, and I didn't know exactly what it was, but I knew I could not fix it by myself. So I found some help, and the problem was fixed, and my life has never been the same since." He did not use a single religious word. But here was what happened. His grandkid's questions came rolling in. For example, he asked, "Grandpa, what was wrong with you?"

"I did some bad things and learned that God didn't like that. He called what I did *sin*."

"Why couldn't you help yourself, Grandpa?"

"Well, I read that there is nothing I could ever do to get rid of my sin by myself. I could not pay anybody to get rid of it. I could not work to get rid of it. And only God could take it away. It's called forgiveness. So I asked Him. And He did it!"

And the questions may get harder, Grandpa, but answer them according to how they apply to you.

Grandpa was not terrifically religious, but he explained the rest of his story. He asked God to forgive him, and he accepted His forgiveness and promised not to do those bad things on purpose again. How did that change this Grandpa's life? This Grandpa serves God, obeys Him, prays to Him, and lives life according to His teachings.

Grandpa, this isn't preaching. It's something that you may be faced with someday. And your grandkids love and trust you so much, they will want an answer. You may have to buck up and take the lumps. It's really important. Be prepared.

Discipline

Discipline does not always need to be administered with a belt, a hickory switch, or a smack with your hand on the buttocks.

Discipline is teaching someone to obey rules or to develop a behavior. Sometimes controlling the actions may involve punishment by restriction or by physical contact. It is a mode of behavior (obeying the rules and becoming trained) that is obtained by cognitive learning or repetition.

The end purpose is to shape and form an individual into compliance.

Furthermore, the reasoning for discipline is rooted in love or admiration. For example, an advanced student disciplines himself to become a scholar by denying himself certain privileges and rewards. If the pupil does not become studious and earns superior grades, those in authority over him may deny him even more of those privileges and rewards until he conforms to a certain behavior.

In other instances, a child may be disobedient or break some rules. His parents may control and punish him by using a belt to teach him and motivate him not to break rules. Grandpa told of the use of a hickory switch on his bare legs back in the day. He said he learned lessons quickly if he wanted to avoid the discipline.

Discipline is good. It is not without pain in many instances, but it is applied for the good of the recipient.

So what is the parents' thinking behind switching their children on their bare legs because they love them?

Grandpa explains that love comes in the form of a sincere desire to raise their children to become good, productive, and law-abiding citizens. And parental discipline helps the parents relate to their children a desire for the children to grow up in a proper manner.

So what is the role of Grandpa in discipline? It is not to punish your grandkids. It is not your responsibility to set or interfere in the pathway of raising your grandkids. That is the job of the parents.

But Grandpa can be a vital part of disciplining your grandkids by building a relationship with them that calls for respect, love, and a willingness to be obedient to rules. Your technique is best served by gentleness, love, and logic. The demonstration of your love for them is foremost seen in the example of your life and your testimony of growing up, having to work at obeying the rules and laws. You can testify as to the love and concern that was shown by your parents.

Discipline by physical punishment may have its place, and Grandpa can lovingly support that style. But your grandkids understand your style too.

Grandpa told the story of him doing some bad things when he was a kid, and he was disciplined for doing them. His mom and dad took something he really loved to do and used it as punishment, like baseball. They never took playing baseball away from him, but his punishment was to have his mother accompany him to practice every day and sit in the stands and watch. And all this was done in front of his friends. Then when they got home, he was restricted to the backyard for a month, except to practice and play games. He said that hurt him very badly, and he learned to never cuss at adults or smoke cigarettes again.

Grandpa said he looked back on those times and realized how much his parents loved him. What they did was hard for them to do, but they knew it was a part of life that paid off.

Dating For Grandkids

The grandkids were amazed. Here was their Grandpa sitting on the swing on the front porch, and all of a sudden, he started talking to them about pretty girls and big hunks. Wow!

"Yessir, I sure am glad God invented beautiful girls and boys who are big hunks. There is nothing finer than to see a big hunk pass by or look at a cool chick." He smiled. "That's the best of life. But you need to remember when you get the tingles, it's not true love." The grandkids felt the warmth of an embarrassing red face.

Time with Grandpa on the porch was about to become a classic.

"What are the tingles, Grandpa?"

Well, that's when you feel fuzzy all over when you see somebody from the opposite sex. You get the tingles and think you may be in love. The tingles is the way God made our bodies. When we get excited, we are overcome with a case of the tingles. So here is what to do when that hunk or that babe becomes your friend and wants to go out with you.

Ask yourself, "How can I get to know him or her better, and what is important and why?"

Well, kids, *The Grandpa's Manual* says three things about matching up with a hunk or a babe, and here they are.

First, ask questions before you get serious and search until you find out if your spirits match. If you have the same spirit, your relationship may just go somewhere. If you do not have the same spirit and still think your babe or your hunk gives you the tingles, life could be miserable. One of you may attempt to win the other one over, or you will just forget about it. It's hard to match a spirit of loving sports with someone who does not like any athletics. It's difficult for two people to become a match when one likes quilting and the other would rather go to the racetrack. Like spirits are more important than some people think. Your faith spirit is very important too. Matching spirits of faith will guide your future.

Second, when you see your spirits match, you may want to continue seeing each other or even think about marriage. Work on your mindset. Where should you live? Should it be close to home or far away? Will the wife work or raise kids? Do you like kids and want to have them around? What hobbies or other interests can you do together? Things like that.

And then when everything gets all mushy and you say the vows, enjoy physical things.

That is the right order of things. Getting them done in the right order really is essential.

"I remember when I met your grandma," Grandpa said as he looked toward the sky with that puppy love expression on his face. "There she was in her three-piece swimming suit standing next to a beach ball. I got a real case of the tingles and could only say two words: hubba-hubba!"

Pets And Heaven

Grandpa, grandkids love their pets almost as much, or more, than they love anything else in the world. That includes their little brother, cheesecake, and you. One of the saddest days in their life will come when their pet no longer lives. It can result in a broken heart, and your grandkid will need comfort in a very special way. Chances are, they will ask a few questions about the incident when they come to you for comfort. Be gentle with them. It's important.

They may ask you a bundle of questions. Let's deal with just one question that will probably top their list: Will my pet go to Heaven?

First, as always, be honest with them. If you do not know the answer, perhaps you may want to begin with a question, such as "What do you think?" At this point, you may anticipate the answer will be "Yes" or "I hope so." This answer can set the stage. So here are a few things you may consider.

The truth of the matter is we do not know for sure that animals go to Heaven. But we sure hope they do, and this is why. Heaven is a place. It's not just a theory in our minds. It is real. It is a place where only happiness exists. There is no sadness in Heaven. The sick and the crippled are all made well, and nobody cries.

We don't exactly know how that happens, but it does. God is in Heaven, and He made it that way. In Heaven, we will know each other, and that will be so happy. The things we did and said on earth will all be forgotten, especially bad and sad things. We will have new minds and new bodies. That's just the way it is.

Now, what about your dog? Again, we don't know if he will be in our Heaven. But we like to think that maybe there is a Doggie Heaven where dogs go and are happy all the time. It is a place for dogs only. There will be no people. And we hope it is where dogs will recognize their doggie friends and will run and play all day with no more sickness for them. They will have plenty to eat, have no leashes, and have lots of couches to lay on; and it will be a place with an abundance of fire hydrants.

What does that do for us when we know this? It makes us happy that our dog will be taken care of. He will have all he needs, and there will be no dog catchers around. We won't see each other again, but that can be okay. When we were together, we brought happiness and joy to each other. And we taught each other stuff, not just tricks. And when it came time for us to separate from each other, it was really sad. It is still sad, but it won't last forever.

You know, we don't know any of this for sure. But what we do know is there is hope. We hope this is the way it will be. One day, we will absolutely know for sure about our pets, and we can hope everything will be all right for them. Meanwhile, we have our own hope about Heaven, and we can know for sure what it is like.

Maybe when it is our time to go to Heaven, we can sit all day under a tree and think about dogs. And at the same time, dogs are lying on the couch in Doggie Heaven thinking about people.

GRANDPA AS A TEACHER

Meeting People

Meeting people is a skill. For example, you may have to learn how to shake hands.

The best way to teach your grandkids how to properly shake hands with meaning is to have a handshaking session.

"Okay, when we shake hands with a person, we want to let them know we are sincere," Grandpa begins. "Who would want to receive your limp handshake? It feels like dead fish."

Handshakes are to be firm. Shaking hands sends a message that says, "I am sincerely happy to make your acquaintance."

When you make a firm handshake, you apply just enough pressure so your hand is not limp. If you squeeze like a vise, the other person may try to match you and break your hand. And if you don't apply any pressure, you're a dead fish.

So practice shaking hands for a few minutes.

Grandpa added, "And make sure you look the person in the eye. It makes a connection with them. Especially when you maintain your firm grip and look them in the eye while you are speaking. Looking away signifies a lack of interest in the person. It's a lack of sincerity." If you want to show added sincerity in your handshake, simply touch the man's forearm gently as you shake his hand. This is acceptable if you are meeting for the first time. If you are meeting more casually or you have met the person before, it may be acceptable to place your hand on his shoulder.

It is impolite and socially incorrect to shake the hand of a woman unless she offers her hand to you. Do not extend your hand first to a lady. If she does not offer her hand to you, simply look her in the eye and acknowledge her presence with a nod of your head. Smile.

It is improper to shake anyone's hand while sitting. Women traditionally are not required to stand. They may shake hands while seated. Again, do not hesitate to greet a lady just because she is sitting down. If she does not extend her hand then just nod. It is gentlemanly to make eye contact with a non-handshaking woman.

Good communication and sincerity go a long way when you are meeting people.

Teaching To Drive A Car

There are some things Grandpas need to know about if and when.

For instance, it is not a matter of if you teach your grandkids to drive a car, it is a matter of when their mom or dad will tell you it's your time on the passenger's side with their son or daughter at the steering wheel, and good luck.

Chances are, you have been blessed with the task of teaching your little angels how to drive a car because their parents are scared out of their wits and fear death. But this is nothing to be afraid of. You have been driving a car since Henry Ford was a pup, and you have been initiated into the great society of Showing the Kids How to Drive.

It may or may not be significant to the young driver, but as you attempt to get off on the right foot, remind him or her that driving is not a right; it is a privilege that must be earned. Driving a car does not appear in the Constitution or the Bible.

There are a few things to watch out for as you begin. First, these grandkids are not of the Henry Ford generation. They dreamed of the day when they could push a muscle car to its limits. They watched *The Italian Job* movie and know how to maneuver a Mini Cooper through the sewers of New York. These kids are inspired by the likes of Joey Chitwood and other stunt drivers.

That is until they buckle up and realize Grandpa is sitting next to them, and this is no dream.

Just gently remind your student driver that this is not a movie, and everything will be okay. We all will die sometime.

Make sure the car you use belongs to somebody else. You don't want your classic Impala weaving down the road with an acne-faced kid peeking over the steering wheel just daring the oncoming traffic to get out of the way. This is the best time to use their parents' car. Just make sure the insurance is paid up and you are carrying your Medicare card.

Be assured that this is nothing to get nervous about. The kid will undoubtedly announce that he already knows everything there is to know about driving. You just need to make sure you are braced and in a position to bail if you have to. So have them start the car. Remind them it is not a good idea to keep grinding the starter. The car will start with a short twist of the key. Put it in gear. If the car has automatic transmission, you're in luck. If it is stick shift, pray harder. Let's assume it's an automatic.

Drive out toward the street. This is a good time to mention looking both ways before turning. But also stress that they are not to look from the middle of the road. Stay put until the way is clear. Signal, turn, give it some gas, and take us down the road. Next, pull over for the nice policeman who is following us with his red lights on. Stay in the car, be quiet, and let Grandpa do the talking.

Now, since that part is taken care of (the cop is a lodge buddy), we can proceed to exiting the freeway. The best way to handle this is to keep it under seventy miles per hour when on the exit ramp and not to come to a sudden stop.

Look both ways, signal, and turn. It's not necessary to drop by the hospital on the way home. Grandpa is okay. He almost always sweats when he thinks he is about to die.

Home at last. Half of the people in the car are joyful and happy. Mom and Dad come prancing out and want to know how everything went. Of course, the stories of the cop and the grinding of gears (the student driver put it in park while rolling to a stop) are embellished a little.

Grandpa tells them the sweat on his brow appears as they learned to use the heater and the air conditioner as part of the lesson. He then smiles nervously.

Grandpa, sometimes you have to do what you have to do. And that can be fun too.

God

God is a subject most people do not like to discuss with relatives or strangers. And rightfully so. It can be uncomfortable at times and extremely intimidating even for churchgoers and religious people. There are debates about God and who He is, where He comes from, and what He does. Fights have even erupted in the churches and synagogues over religious things. But sometimes, Grandpas need to buck up and do uncomfortable things for the betterment of their grandkids. Again, honesty is the best policy. One day, a grandkid may ask you about God. So you tell that precious little soul what you know. That's it. If you don't know much, say so.

Let's share three helpful things about God without sounding like we are at a church service. Each bit of information deals with a common concept you may hear during a discussion at any coffee shop, bar, or lunchroom.

First, the Bible teaches that there is only one God. He created everything that was ever created. The world, animals, people, the sky, the ocean, cats, and little sisters. That same God loves everyone, period. It doesn't matter how mean they are or what they did, He loves them just the same. His desire is that they have a high quality of life that supersedes being mean and bad. So He tells us about it. It's in the Bible.

Second, there are gods made out of wood and stone and jewels and stuff. They are not alive, and they never made anything. But people believe in them and worship them and pray to them. Who they are and what they do was made up by some guy somewhere who wrote a book about it. People read it and liked it, so they followed the teachings. By the way, that's in the Bible too.

Third, there are gods that can be found anywhere. They look like things. Whatever the things are, they become powerful in the sight of some people who dedicate their lives to those things. They don't necessarily pray to those gods, but instead, they love those gods and play games with them and put other gods out of their minds. They are not interested in a high quality of life or utopia when they die. It's not important to them. What they believe is in the Bible too.

Grandpa, you don't have to be religious or a Bible scholar to share that information with your grandkids. But what is important is to read the Bible where those gods are written about so you can better answer your grandkid's questions.

You may not always have the answers. It's better to find the answer and be prepared than to skip the question. Use the Bible as your best reference to help find the answer. Most likely, your grandkid's confidence will be renewed by knowing that his Grandpa has the answer to those questions too.

Here are a few references from the Bible that may help you:

- Genesis 1, 2, and 3—God made everything.
- Romans 1:18–32 (note verses 21–23)—other gods were made.
- Exodus 20:3 (note this is the first of the Ten Commandments)—don't have any other gods before you.

Prayer

It's not unusual to pray. There are multitudes of people who pray that don't even believe in God. But they pray all the time.

So why is it important for Grandpas to teach their grandkids about praying?

Prayer is a unique thing. Nonreligious people and religious fanatics alike know that there is something about prayer that soothes the soul and calms them down. There will be a time when your grandkids will ask you about prayer and the reason we should pray. What do you tell them? Start with the truth.

Prayer is a means of communication. In the spiritual realm, of course, prayer is us communicating with God. But there are some people who pray to other people, or idols, or philosophies, or nothing. They just pray. Some say there will always be prayer in our schools as long as there are tests.

The truth of the matter is prayer involves a desire to communicate with a higher being. If it is the God of the Bible, a person's spirit can be lifted, and he can see and understand the multifaceted elements of prayer to God. If we communicate with prayer to other people or things, we need to understand that our prayers are said for a myriad of reasons and may not line up with teaching of the Bible.

Nevertheless, prayer is important to most everybody. Even people who do not want to have anything to do with prayer can produce a reason for not praying.

So our grandchildren are inquisitive. They should be taught that prayer is not a shopping list, where they ask for things they do not have. Neither is it a super hyped method of being cured or healed. It is communication. When we pray, we communicate by speaking our mind and revealing our spirit and heart. It makes us satisfied that we have personally communicated with someone or something bigger than us. The beauty of praying is that anybody can do it, not just grandkids. Prayer is something for people of all ages, nationalities, and beliefs to share.

Some Grandpas feel it is their duty and privilege to tell their grandkids about prayer. Remember, be honest and open with them because grandkids know when their Grandpa is faking it. Tell them what you know.

Reading

It has been said that if a person reads books for thirty minutes in one particular subject, he can become an expert on that topic in one month. That makes sense. Concentration on one topic for a certain length of time will certainly help you become very familiar with that subject.

Reading is important. A well-read person is, in sorts, self-educated.

Grandpas know that encouraging their grandkids to read can expand their minds, open up new fields of interest, sharpen their understanding of things that they are passionate about, and create dreams and fantasies worth pursuing.

Books are a mystic wonderland that opens the eyes of your grandkids and grooms them to be able to converse with strangers and teachers alike. You may be a great source of learning, but books are a wider source of wisdom and information that you may not be able to shed light upon. Books span a wide range of subjects that can open the minds of children and adults alike. Encourage your grandkids to read. Read with them. Share the same book and discuss it with them later. In doing so, you may develop your own love for reading. You can become a serious, never-ending source of companionship to your grandkids as you read together.

Teach your grandkids how to select the books they read. Suggest to them that choosing books is like choosing their friends. The reader and the book should have something in common so they can feel good about spending time together. Just as you seek out new friends, also explore new books.

Having a favorite author is important, but challenge your grandkids to read books by different authors. Who knows, they may accumulate a list of favorite writers.

Reading is a great teaching tool. Bonding with your grandkids by reading uses that tool to build and strengthen your relationship.

GRANDPA'S WISDOM

Listen To Grandma

Listen to Grandma.

This includes Grandpa, your children, your grandchildren, the PTA, all the neighbors, the newspapers, and the local radio station.

Grandma is a wonderful person filled with wisdom, grace, and advice. Quite often, she is willing to offer her insight, especially if it will preserve the safety and well-being of her family and friends. She, too, has walked the long road of life along with all its bumps and curves. Now she is ready to share her journey with her family and friends. The trek was worth it.

Her wisdom comes from raising Grandpa. Raising him would surely increase anybody's grace and wisdom, not to mention their patience. She has the advantage from the start when he announced that he wanted to be a kid when he grew up. Over the course of their half century of marriage, she has watched as his desires adjusted. With tongue in cheek, she just smiles and says, "I often wonder what he will be if he grows up." She knows Grandpa better than anyone in the world. And with that familiarity comes increased wit and wisdom. When he has a hankering to do something crazy with the grandkids, he better check with Grandma first. If she advises him not to do something because he is going to hurt himself, he usually gives it a second thought because he is going to hurt himself.

And if she tells the story to the grandkids about the little boy or girl who would not eat everything on their plate and what happened to them, it's just better to clean their plates.

Grandkids catch on fast. If an idea sounds the least bit questionable, you can bet one of them will say, "Have you checked with Grandma yet?" It doesn't matter how smart and slick you think you are, one way or the other, Grandma is the go-to person.

She has intuition. She can predict things. She warned Grandpa not to go down the waterslide with the grandkids or he would not be able to get out of bed in the morning. Sure enough, he not only went down the waterslide, but he drew an audience when he tried to show off. He got a standing ovation when he dove headfirst and somersaulted all the way to the bottom. The grandkids were the talk of the day at the water park. Kids and parents alike said they admired how cool Grandpa was. And he loved it. It took him three days to get out of bed because of the pain.

But Grandma took good care of him and never said a discouraging word. She just smiled.

When the grandkids announced that Grandpa was going to get on a motorcycle and enter the Widow Maker hill climb, she couldn't believe it. So she went along, set up her chair at the bottom of the giant hill, and just waited for his name to be called. He rode by and solicited a good luck kiss from her. She kissed him back and whispered in his ear.

The whistle blew, Grandpa jumped back on his borrowed bike, revved the engine, and took off at full speed. He was just about to the top of the hill when he suddenly realized he was in the wrong gear and obviously was not going to make it to the top. In that position, experienced hill-climbing bikers would tell you not to just get off the bike. You were 150 yards straight up.

He got off the bike.

To his chagrin, he decided even before he reached the bottom of the hill that he should have practiced more. So there he was, still breathing and slightly moaning. Nobody touched him, for it was obvious what happened. They called 911, and Grandma met them at the hospital.

So what did she whisper in his ear? "There's still time to back out, and I'm here for you."

If you fail to listen to Grandma, you won't always meet with tragedy. But if you do, Grandma will be the first to be there. She knows the value of loving-kindness. She predicts the good and bad. She is the balance that Grandpa needs for his every quest to become the oldest kid on the block.

Listen to Grandma. She knows.

The Value Of A Regular Routine

Grandpa, sometimes there can be methods in your madness. Take for instance going to bed at the same time every night. As we get older, it may be a necessity rather than a disciplined choice. Doing yard work, lifting rocks, and hauling gravel may make a regular bedtime look even sweeter. Most of the time, a good dose of anti-hurt-all-over pills mixed with a few extra-strength gee-I-shouldn't-have-wheeled-that-cart-across-the-lawn tablets is a wonderful prelude to early slumber. A dip in the spa or a very hot shower wouldn't hurt either.

Most of the family is in agreement with the example you set and wonder why going to bed at the same time every night is so important. Most of them know that an early bedtime is something you have done for years.

Grandpa was having a Blizzard with his granddaughter who was in college. The early bedtime was explained. No matter what the event was the next day, into bed early produces a fresh mind in the morning and mentally prepares you for the day. Falling asleep in the most boring class never happened with Grandpa. And his agenda for the day did not include a nap, not even a little snooze.

Creation of a habit is not the same as being disciplined. The habit is formed when you do something several times over and over again until it becomes a part of your life. Discipline is the way you conform to the habit. So going to bed early is a habit that produces a disciplined life. He said young people need to hear that. College life can be notorious for parties and pulling all-nighters (staying up all night) cramming for a test. But it doesn't need to be that way. Students and their parents pay a lot of money for education, and serious students usually take good advice from wherever they can get it.

His granddaughter made the Dean's Academic List as a freshman. And her Grandpa could not have been prouder. He asked her how she did it. Her reply was that she took his advice and went to bed every night at 10:00 p.m. no matter what. So every day right after classes, she went back to the dorm and did all her homework early so she could relax part of the evening before bedtime.

Whew, a freshman doing homework right after class. He never thought of that when he was a freshman. Of course, when he was young, some students never let their education interfere with their social life.

Grandpa, you never know when grandkids will listen to you, learn, and give you the credit.

Every Dog Should Have A Boy!

Grandpa knows the value of having a canine friend. He raised dozens of dogs during his lifetime and could tell you every one of their names and breed, usually. Most of the dogs were mutts, and he called a couple of them by the same name. One thing is for sure. He is a self-made expert on the notion that every dog needs a kid and every kid needs a dog.

Dogs aren't perfect because they are trained by people who are not perfect. A dog does what he is taught to do. If you don't want a mean dog, don't teach him to be mean. Some dogs are labeled with a bad reputation for being savage guard dogs and mean just because of their breed. That is bogus. Those dogs can be as loving as any other dog. Adopt one of those dogs when he is a pup before he learns bad habits and train him to be nice.

Dogs respond to their surroundings. When they are loved, they love back. When they learn a trick and get a reward, they wag their tails. And if a dog is ignored, misses a feeding, or has to find his own drinking water because boy or girl forgot to fill the water dish, he does not hold a grudge. Dogs don't know any better. They are loyal. They sleep on the floor by the bed, on the bed, or in the bed. They love to play and lick faces.

Grandpa was talking to his grandkid about dogs and asked, "If your dog could do anything in the world, what would it be?"

His grandkid thought for a minute. "Anything? I think I would like to have him understand English and teach me to speak and understand barking."

Little did his grandkid know that dogs can understand English (or any other language). Dog experts tell us that a dog can understand and respond to a whole bunch of words. Grandpa didn't know exactly how many, but he guessed about five hundred.

It takes training, but most dogs can do it. But if you think about it, it takes training for humans to master something too.

Grandpa said he was sure the dog could not teach someone how to bark, but it would be interesting if he could. Nevertheless, he knows and can appreciate what dogs do. Little boys who grow up with their dogs become better people, usually. And there is joy in the life of a dog that has a boy for his very own.

They are just like humans in many ways. Leave it up to Grandpa to pass that bit of wisdom on to his grandkids.

Motorcycles

There are a lot of Grandpas who rode motorcycles when they were younger. For sure, most of them would admit this was a fine way to get around, especially if Grandma was leaning against the sissy bar right behind them. There was nothing better than zooming along the freeway then taking the exit ramp and splitting off into the wheatlands with all the winding roads, leaning into corners and having bugs splatter on your face shield.

One day your grandkid may slip into your place, sidle up to you, and announce he or she wants to get a motorcycle. If you have stories about riding your motorcycle, it's okay to tell them, adding how fun riding a motorcycle can be. But always include the dangers.

Here is what's important: Your grandkid most likely will be coming to you for support. Be careful because this may be a trap. It may be that Mom and Dad already said no.

So what do you do?

First, do not usurp the parents. Don't ever attempt to override the authority or wishes of your grandkid's parents (even if you disagree with them). It's a matter of maintaining and building good relationships and has nothing to do with motorcycles or anything else. It is your job to encourage your grandkids to honor their parents. Sneaking around looking for Grandpa's support is going to be attempted by them. So stick to the higher principle and tell them sneaking around is wrong, period.

Second, it is not Grandpa's place to help finance a motorcycle unless the purchase has been approved and he is willing and able to help finance it. It is not his place to help find a way to buy one or conjure up a plan to obtain one, again, unless the parents give approval.

Third, do not sugarcoat anything when it comes to telling the dangers of riding a motorcycle. Riding a motorcycle is dangerous. The danger in riding is not always about the rider. It's about those motorists and truckers who overlook motorcycle riders and ignore the presence of a bike on the road. It's easy to fall for the old line: "But, Grandpa, I'll be careful and watch out!" It may be offered with sincerity, but it's lame. All the care in the world can't account for stupid, reckless drivers. There are stories galore of experienced motorcycle riders who know the danger of being on two wheels and are excellent riders. But some car or truck does not see them, and the excellent rider is ran over and is crippled or dead. Enrolling in the Riding Academy is important, but it does not erase the dangers.

When you rode a motorcycle you might have found it necessary to lay your bike down. You might have crashed one. It behooves you to be honest and open with the ones you love so much. They will try to make a good case for buying a motorcycle. You might have loved your motorcycle, and obviously, you are not dead; but think it through. Protect your grandkids from making what may turn out to be a very unwise decision.

GRANDPA'S LOVE

Troubles

Grandpa, you can be a pillar of comfort when your grand-kid comes to you with a troubled heart and emotions that may disrupt his life. He can find comfort in just knowing that the warmth and concern you give to him is the kind of comfort he can use to comfort others. He can depend on you.

In your walk along that road of life, you may have covered enough distance to know that troubled hearts and spirits cannot be fixed instantly or ordered away. The one who is bearing a difficult burden may be seeking comfort in order to move on.

When your grandkid is hurting and is feeling the anxieties of life, he should know that his Grandpa can be the one who will hug him and whisper to him some assurance of his love. His confidence usually comes when you make yourself available to help work things out. Grandkids need to know that disappointments, troubled hearts, and anxieties will creep into their lives. They may have heard that it's not the troubles and anxieties that will necessarily shape their lives. It is the way they react to them and deal with them that will play a major role in forming who they are. They should be able to depend on your wisdom and love to walk with them through those hardships.

Grandpas are not always fixers. Your love and compassion for your grandkid during this difficult time can help heal and mend the bruises. The source of your comfort may be important to you, and perhaps, you may not want to reveal it to him. So gently say to your hurting grandkid, "This, too, will pass!" Take some time and explain to him that a troubled heart and a wounded spirit won't last forever. A young aching heart needs to hear that message, especially from his Grandpa.

Getting All The Ink

Part of a regular day for Grandpa is to pour a cup of coffee and read the newspaper. With the computer age in full swing, newspapers are slowly becoming less and less popular. There is still something special about reading the paper in the morning.

As he reads the newspaper, he says it seems as though grandkids are getting more and more ink for the mean and bad things they do, while the good grandkids kids are getting fewer stories for the good things they accomplish.

Other than the fact that sensationalism sells papers, why are a majority of grandkids being passed over by the media? Our grandkids are very intelligent, creative young people. Many of them seek a cause and dedicate themselves to it. They are imaginative and helpful. Yet fewer and fewer media outlets are recognizing them.

You may not be able to pinpoint the reason for them being ignored, but one certainty remains: Grandpa and rest of the family are proud of them. And the executives in the corporate world, service organizations, and mission groups are seeking out these young people. They are in demand.

It is good that you recognize successes as well as the extreme efforts these grandkids are making. It is not necessary to placate them with unwarranted flattery. Just lift them up with genuine gestures of pride for their accomplishments.

Grandpa, this is important in cementing your relationship with them. Communicate with your grandkids that they are important people and what they are doing is important. You may have missed the opportunities your grandkids have today, so love up on them and encourage them to grab the ball and run with it.

It is also important to realize that not all Grandpas have grandkids who excel. This may be sad, but do not despair. The love of a Grandpa for his grandkids supersedes everything. That includes jail, fights, failed relationships, and the like. Pledge to yourself to never break the bond of love that forms your relationship regardless of the circumstances. Sometimes it will be difficult, and it may seem hopeless. Hang in there because it's important for them to know that no matter what, Grandpa still loves them.

Stories in the newspaper are nice. It's good to see their names in ink. But it's better to celebrate with your grandkids the relationships and accomplishments they have made.

Perseverance

Grandpa, who could be more persevering than a one-armed baseball player? One grandkid told about his Grandpa who taught him how to persevere even when things seemed a little dark.

His Grandpa was a farmer. As a small child, he caught his hand in a meat grinder. He never considered himself to be handicapped. He seemed as normal as the kids around him. It wasn't long before he excelled on the playground, the classroom, and later, the sports arena. He played baseball, basketball, and football all through high school and even won some awards. Often, he was chosen by local service organizations to be a keynote speaker, telling about how he persevered through life. He would tell them it wasn't difficult for him because he never knew what normal was. He barely recalled ever having two hands.

He demonstrated how he pitched a baseball. He would carry a baseball glove in his car, knowing somebody would sooner or later ask him how he did it. "Well, I just gripped my glove under my left arm. I would wind up and pitch the ball and almost at the same time slip the glove on my right hand and be ready to field the ball. It's not a complicated thing to do, but it does take a lot of practice."

Later on, Grandpa learned about a man named Jim Abbott who made it to the Major Leagues as a pitcher. He had one arm and used the same technique.

Grandpa and his grandkid lived together after the boy's dad died. Grandpa was young at the time and not very grandfatherly. But he taught many principles of life that have remained in the mind of his grandkid to this day.

Grandpa was not a patient person. He yelled a lot when things were tense. But he settled down when he realized that the example he was setting for his grandkid was not a very good one. So he became gentler and even more caring. He was a very hard worker and knew the value of hard work. He taught by example.

He and his grandkid had a very close relationship. Once, the grandkid scolded him and accused him of not knowing how to be a Grandpa. There was a hesitation, and the room was silent. Oops, had the grandkid spoken out of line? Maybe he even hurt Grandpa's feelings. Grandpa just stared at him. Then he spoke. "Oh yeah? Well, you better take some lessons on how to be a grandson!"

Silence again. What can you say after that? They slowly approached each other and hugged. Instead of apologizing, Grandpa just hugged tighter. In the hug came the clear message that Grandpa loved that kid very much. The grandkid got the message. That was just the way it was.

Life is full of hard times. They come and they go. Some stick around. Persevering is a learned skill that comes from other disciplines, like caring about people and having a respect for their feelings. It comes from maturity and knowing what makes up your worldview. Persevering takes practice, and the reward is commensurate with how hard you practice.

Grandpa, this may be difficult for your grandkid to wrap his head around. So maybe an easier approach would be to say, "When things get tough, hang in there. You'll be glad you did!"

Teaching Or Encouraging?

Without a doubt, Grandpas need to encourage their grandkids whenever the occasion arises. There are some times when teaching can't be distinguished from encouraging, and they become one and the same.

Grandpa invited his grandkids to sleep over one night. He simply wanted to talk and maybe share a story or two. Both of them wanted to get to know each other better.

"So, Grandpa, what are we having for breakfast?" the grandkid asked.

Grandpa thought about it for a minute and replied, "Hotcakes would be nice. Would you like to help me make them?"

They went to the kitchen counter, pulled out all the ingredients for making hotcakes, and began to create. Grandpa started to get the feeling that this could be a teaching moment, so he gave his spiel. Knowing that this could be far more than just a lesson in cooking, Grandpa told his cook apprentice that he preferred some fresh fruit mixed in his hotcakes. All the ingredients were whipped to perfection.

"Now, what kind of fruit do you think would go good in these hotcakes, son?" Grandpa asked.

It took a minute, but the answer was "Whatever kind you have in the refrigerator, Grandpa!" And it was obvious the lad was beginning to enjoy being a student as well as a grandkid.

"Exactly right, young man. Let's take a look."

It did not take long to finish the job. It was an opportune time for Grandpa to encourage his grandson, who did not need to be criticized. Grandpa figured this young boy probably received enough of that at school and maybe at home. So with each step, Grandpa Chef complimented the hotcake maker. And with each compliment came an extra dose of enthusiasm, even some creativity.

And there it was, a stack of near-perfect tomato hot-cakes garnished with a couple slices of cucumber. Grandpa had forgotten to put fresh fruit in the fridge and had just stocked it with veggies from the garden. True, they were the most unusual hotcakes ever served, but they demanded praise, not for the taste particularly but for the fact that this grandkid was encouraged to be innovative when creating something on his own. His self-esteem went up more than a couple notches. And Grandpa kept reminding himself that no matter what they make, eat it.

Nicknames

What do your grandkids call you? It's interesting to hear all the nicknames they come up with. We never did figure out where he got the name, but we called our Grandpa "Slick." We just guessed he got the name because he was bald, and that was what everyone called him. He was a miner in the Ozark Mountains, and we suspect those hillbillies in the galena mines pinned it on him.

Anyway, he let us call him Slick. To him, it was a term of endearment.

Grandpas and grandmas have special names, and most of them were chosen by the grandkids. Usually, the parents selected the moniker long before their children could walk or talk. New parents probably introduced their babies to you and Grandma when the grandkids were a few hours old. It took a couple years for the grandkids to recognize you and remember your name. Before the grandkids could talk, they just cried. The only thing they were interested in was having you pick them up so they could wet on you. When your special name came later in life (most likely it changed from the original), the best thing you could do was to let them use it and enjoy it. The name was devised out of love for you, and it is special to them. Sometimes a name is developed by the grandkid's inability to properly speak the king's English. Names like Pah-ah or Pawnee or something that sounds like a loving term of endearment but cannot be interpreted. Let that go too. It will work itself out.

In one way or another, those special names have personal meaning for the grandkids. They want to be close to you, and the name they call you helps them do that. After all, who would want their grandkid to call them Charles, Lester, or Hank?

Some Grandpas have responded to names like Hawky (or Hockey, we didn't know which was which) and Beatle Barn and Snicker-doo. A couple favorites include Graham Cracker and Poppy. One couple said they are known as Gump and Bubbles.

Having a custom name is one of the special privileges of being a Grandpa. Let your grandkids choose your nickname and accept it no matter what it is. It's their way of loving you.

It's in the Manual

Grandpa had a unique sense of humor. He was a type-A personality. Actually, he was quite a fun-loving man, and the grandkids adored him. On any given day, folks in the community could see him walking his cat on a leash or sitting on a park bench with his Cockatoo on his shoulder eating peanuts as the shells dropped all over his jacket.

So it was no wonder when something that was unpleasant but necessary had to be done he would announce, "Grandpa will do it because it's in the manual!" There was no actual manual, but Grandpa told everybody there was. One day, the energy and wisdom packed between his ears would escape and folks would better understand the beauty and challenges of being a Grandpa.

That being said, it was time to pull his grandkids first loose tooth.

It had lingered in his mouth much too long. The young owner was scared out of his wits. It just hung there almost daring somebody to pull it out. For the grandkid, it was a first-time experience. Most of the family members balked. A volunteer was hard to find. Usually, a five- or six-year-old child will not trust anyone to perform this ritual. Mom and Dad worked overtime offering comfort. Brother and sister were not asked because they would have refused anyway.

Grandpa may have had the edge. His technique was to begin by sitting the anxious child down and explaining that the tooth needed to come out so the new tooth could grow in its place. Plus, the tooth fairy had an abundance of reward money just waiting to be slipped under the pillow in exchange for the old tooth.

So Grandpa began. His primary mode of operation had been criticized for years by generations. It was simple. He tied one end of a string to the doorknob and the other end to the tooth and slammed the door. Usually that worked best if the grandkid completely trusted Grandpa and there was no pain involved. But the slightest flinch or an attempted movement toward the door by the grandkid put an end to Grandpa's great technique. So he was faced with crisis management. Grandpa explained the calming ritual he performed with his grandkid before Plan B could be initiated.

He reassured the youngster by telling stories of how this would not hurt a bit. He promised the snaggletoothed kid it would all be over in an instant. The sobbing child protected himself with both hands, refusing to let Grandpa go anywhere near his mouth with another piece of string. Grandpa admitted it usually took him a few dollar bills or some candy to get the procedure started.

He was experienced. Still there was no comfort for the kid in knowing his Grandpa yanked out dozens of teeth belonging to the poor child's relatives.

First, Grandpa promised the dental floss would never touch the doorknob. Second, there would be no pulling. These were promises on which Grandpa staked his life. This tooth was a very loose tooth. There was a small space between the tooth and the gum tissue on the tongue side of the tooth. So Grandpa placed the dental floss around the tooth and with a spoon handle slipped the floss into that space under the tooth. With the utmost care, he guided the floss between the teeth and crossed it on the front side of the tooth. He then gently tightened the two ends of the floss. There was no pulling involved. The tooth was out in an instant, and the job was done!

Grandpa was extremely gentle and reassuring, all the while talking and whispering to his patient. The grandkid hardly even noticed what was being done.

"Now, one more time," Grandpa said. "Let's take a look in the mirror and see that tooth."

"Oh, my goodness, where is my tooth?" his grand-kid shouted. As they both broke out in laughter, Grandpa showed his grandkid the tooth he had hidden in the palm of his hand.

The whole procedure lifted Grandpa to another level of trust in the eyes of the toothless kid.

"The next procedure is to get a small plastic lunch bag, place the tooth in it, and find your pillow," Grandpa instructed. "It's a rule that we both have to place it in the bag and under the pillow together. Then we can get a bowl of chocolate ice cream with nuts and whipped cream. It's in the manual."

GRANDPA'S TRADITIONS

Apple Picking

Grandpa, you and Grandma are the chief organizers for the annual apple-picking adventure at the local orchard. It's your job to make sure everybody is present and knows the route. In a caravan of four to five cars, it's not unusual for one of them to get separated. Cell phones are used to stay in contact. The latest adventure went like clockwork.

The first stop was the family's favorite espresso stand. For the grandkids, it was a place to order their favorite non-coffee drinks and let everyone know we were headed to the apple orchard for the day. Grandpa called it "the giggle stop." For the adults, it was time to put a little blood in their caffeine streams and proudly show off their family.

Fully present, the clan numbered fifteen. The tradition was for Grandpa to foot the bill. He jokingly reminded everyone that he was digging into their inheritance and that they should enjoy their treat. Secretly, he usually paid for anybody's drink who expressed admiration for such a beautiful-looking family. He just burst with pride as he shuffled them in line. He usually added to the fun by referring to them as part of the family.

Next was the picture ritual. Grandpa volunteered to snap the photo but was reminded he needed to be in the picture. So a bystander jumped in and helped. His coffee was free, too, of course.

At the orchard, everyone gathered for the apple-picking rules. The grandkids seemed to be oblivious to the instructions and wildly started snapping apples off the trees. It must have been the rush of adrenaline they got from imagining that the whole orchard was theirs.

Every grandkid grabbed a sack or a box and moved out helter-skelter for the trees. Most of them could not tell one apple from the other, so they had to be corralled by their parents. If left unsupervised, the boxes could have easily been filled with dozens of apples representing every kind and color.

Meanwhile, Grandpa was calculating the bill.

For the little ones, apples with worms had no significance. Into the bag they went. For the older kids, it was the bigger, the better. Of course, Grandpa tried to be subtle: "Oh my, that sure looks like a lot of apples. Are you sure you can eat that many?" The grandkids missed the hint altogether and kept picking. The parents reminded him that his hint was not very subtle.

The fellowship was great. Lessons on thriftiness and moderation went right out the window. All the adults had no trouble reminding Grandpa who would be picking up the bill. He playfully grumbled under his breath. It was like a ritual. The grandkids had the time of their lives.

It was checkout time, and the scales lit up for everyone to see almost one hundred pounds of apples. Most of the onlookers had been clued in, so they applauded and cheered as Grandpa pulled out his wallet. He took a bow and instructed each grandkid to select an all-day sucker as he, once again, dipped into their inheritance. It was worth it.

That Deserves A Blizzard

Investments are not always made on Wall Street. One Grandpa declared that he "never spent a dime on his grandkids." He said he made investments in them. For instance, there are times when the entire family heads out to the local Dairy Queen for a Blizzard. It's not an every-day occurrence. It's a special time when somebody in the family does something great. It's a battle cry. When it is blurted out, the cheers go up, jumping and shouting usually rocks the place, and there is a lot of handshaking and backslapping. Somebody in the family has accomplished an extremely monumental task. One of the grandkids took a test in a subject he was struggling with and got an A, or someone graduated from college with an advanced degree. It might even be that an accomplished musician in the family finished a concert or a recital. No matter what it may have been, everyone knows the next stop is Dairy Queen and a Blizzard. But more importantly, the entire family is proud of the accomplishment, and that usually results in strong family unity and support. Combined with excellence in performance and wild celebration, the whooping and shouting is a sign of love and appreciation.

Grandpa usually pays the bill while being self-assured that his investment will pay great and lasting dividends.

Sucking ice cream through a straw is not just a reward. It is a gathering. It is an unembarrassed public display of unity and happiness. It's a great tradition.

You may want to consider starting a tradition in your family. It'll pay off.

At The Auction

Have you ever taken one or more of your grandkids to an auction?

There seems to be something about the atmosphere at an auction that encourages people to sit on rock-hard folding chairs or bleachers in a crowded room permeated with the aroma of chili and nacho cheese. Then they see how one can outsmart the other for the privilege of giving away their money. It's a sport, and the good bidders do their homework and have a playbook.

It's a good idea to get to the auction early so you see and test all the merchandise. What may appear to look new and bright from afar may need to be examined closely before the evening's bidding wars begin. There must be a reason for a box of old hoses and a bundle of taped-up lawn tools being pushed to the back of the pre-auction table. So encourage your grandkids to check out what they may like to own. Remind them that the whole deal will appear much differently from ten rows back with people yelling and dancing.

There is usually a bidding strategy. Rookies and little kids don't always know that if they "scratch their nose or fix their hair" at an auction, they may wind up with a box of dented pie plates or a collection of classic books with some pages missing. So it may be wise to tell them that you will be doing all the bidding at first.

Explain to your grandkids that to avoid taking home a rusty refrigerator or a lawn cart with a missing wheel, you have to be fast. If you are in the game for the sport and are attempting to psych out the opponent by raising the bidding bar, bidding first, and keeping it low, Focus is essential, so tell them not to bother you or ask questions until the bidding has stopped. Once the auctioneer slams down the gavel and shouts "Sold!" it's too late.

Just to please your anxious grandkids, do not lose your focus. One Grandpa lost his focus and ended up buying a dented, pedal-powered fire engine with chipped paint.

Grandpa noted the next item had been examined on the pre-auction table. It was a model racing airplane. "Remember," Grandpa reminded them, "be fast!"

The bidding started with one dollar shouted from the back of the room.

"Do you want this? Quick, quick, tell me."

Grandpa wasn't quite yelling, but he was obviously anxious.

Sonny couldn't speak.

"Quick, quick, the bidding is moving, and it's going to be sold."

"Well, it seems like it would be fun, and Joey has a red one, but I don't know."

"Quick, it's going fast."

"Sold!"

"Yeah, I want it," he informed Grandpa with such excitement. "Sorry about that," Grandpa informed him, and the bidding on the next item began before anyone had time to cry or pout.

At the end of the event, some of the commercial buyers shook hands and vowed to see each other next week. They continued their bidding wars in the parking lot, reinspecting the bargains and making offers to trade or buy.

The kids were allowed to try their hand at bidding on the miscellaneous boxes at the end of the night. The segment usually began with one of the kids bidding a dime. The limit was a dollar. Nobody ever exceeded it.

Coming home and bragging about what they had done, all the merchandise was spread out on the kitchen table.

"Gee, for a buck, we won the mystery box!" Included in it was an old egg beater, three canning jars, a small engine for a model airplane, and something that looked like a tool. The second and third boxes were dumped on the table, and the auction-goers stayed up after midnight checking it all out.

Grandma just shook her head, smiled, and left the room.

The Art Of Canning

The canning of fresh fruits and vegetables is a foreign activity for most grandkids. It is a skill that is best passed on by Grandma and Grandpa. The fresh food even tastes fresher if it is harvested from Grandpa's garden. But a trip to the local Farmer's Market is a great way to enhance the canning experience.

It was an awesome sight to see all the beautiful fruits and vegetables displayed in the booths just waiting to be sampled.

Even more fun was listening to Grandpa tell stories about comparing the local farmer's tomatoes with his dad's crops. Grandpa's dad always had the biggest tomatoes. They were called beef steak tomatoes and could be sliced and placed on a dinner plate. Some of them were so big they hung over the side of the plate. The yellow ears of corn were sweeter and easier to shuck. He made sure the farmer was not offended by the comparison, and he always left with a handshake and a glowing compliment to the farmer on his wonderful-looking crop.

Before the canning begins, all the products from the Farmer's Market are evaluated and counted. The amount of food is planned, and certain jars are assigned to that vegetable or fruit. The equipment is hauled out and checked. There are dozens of jars, gigantic kettles, tongs, lids, and sealing rings. Grandma usually makes the announcement that it is time to start. The preparation begins with peeling apples, scraping carrots, and cutting them up. The corn is shucked and cut off the cobs. And there is much more, including washing all those jars, mixing the spices, and boiling water for the jars.

The process appears to be almost sacred. There seem to be little secrets that make Grandma and Grandpa's canning techniques better than the neighbor's.

Some of the grandkids will occasionally attend the home canning activities. They are fascinated by the whole process. Sometimes there are others that are not much interested in being there, but Grandma usually insists, and they stay and watch. Sneaking a sample of the cooked products is a no-no, and your hand could get slapped. It's all part of the ritual. Watching or participating in canning can be a memorable time of bonding for everyone.

Organic fruits and vegetables are the best. Of course, the farmers have them available, but Grandpa likes to grow his own. The entire family is amazed at the size and quality of his organic efforts. Grandpa just grins and is very careful to protect his gardening secrets.

"Yessir," he secretly reveals to his friends, "I'm an organic gardener, but I spray at night!"

Internet Doctors

Grandpa, you may be one of those people who grew up with your mom or dad practicing home remedy medicine. Today's doctors are very well-trained, but some of the home practitioners could probably hold their own when it comes to mixing up and applying mustard plaster or concocting an all-purpose elixir. Back then, the best way to get rid of a boil was to peel an egg and remove the thin skin separating the shell and the inner egg. Then lay it on the boil, and the sore would disappear in a few days. A workable alternative was to scrape a potato and apply it to the boil in the same manner.

As time progresses, so does medicine. Nowadays, grandkids may introduce their Grandpas to the Internet Doctor. Your introduction to the streaming physician may begin with an explanation of how to treat most illnesses with advice found on your computer. The Internet Doctor may even suggest what over-the-counter medication are best. So it's fairly understandable to see why some Grandpas are tuned in to their illnesses before they make an appointment with a real doctor. When Grandpas enter the treatment room and the doctor comes in, it's not uncommon for Grandpas to announce their illness and predict the remedy. An understanding doctor will usually play along with the hoax and ask Grandpa what medical school he attended. Then Grandpa will make a confession that he got the information on the Internet. The doctor usually walks through the advantages of in-person medical diagnosis with his patient. Most of the time, the home remedies are just fine to use, but things like blood pressure and ear, nose, and throat examinations are better performed in the doctor's office.

Ah, the Internet. It's where anyone can Google anything. Grandkids lovingly assure their Grandpas they can find the cure for the symptoms of any illness online.

If six Grandpas were having coffee at the local coffee shop, you might soon discover seven remedies for the same ailment, all found on the Internet. There is no record of any stories having been told about how to remove a tumor or an appendix yet. But you can be sure somebody will try to convince the others that it may be worth a try.

GRANDPA'S EXAMPLE

Role Models

Let's begin by asking you, "Who is your role model?" It could be the one person who had the most influence in your life and is no longer with us, but his lessons and actions live on.

The term *role model* is the brain child of a group of psychologists and sociologists led by Robert Merton, who defines it as "the actions, language, behavior and success of people to whom others aspire to emulate." Athletes seem to fit the category quite well. But not all role models are successful and famous. There are ordinary, common folks who become role models to their children. There are other adults who may make an impact in someone's life and are often found within the circle of influence of your parents or friends.

One grandkid announced that his role model was a famous athlete. The reason was his wealth, his playing ability, and the cool car he drove. The young kid based his admiration for the athlete on things that could easily disappear depending on his batting average or his jump shot. That is understandable. The I-want-to-be-like-Mike era may live on forever. Of course, we are referring to Michael Jordan, the famous basketball player. Many kids think that way.

But what about those men and women who are acclaimed to be role models based on what they believe and how they act outside the sports arena. There are many. Some athletes abuse their role model title and disregard the use of unacceptable words and actions that may influence young developing minds. A lesson for your grandkids is to remind them to be alert to what personal characteristics make someone their role model. Don't emulate those who have broken the law or have done immoral things.

One Grandpa was interviewed and said his role model as a kid was Albert Einstein. He said Einstein was a genius and had a passion for making the world better by inventing things and using his mind. Einstein once said, according to this Grandpa, that he never considered himself a genius. He was disciplined, worked hard, and followed his instincts in discovering even the simplest needs of the world. What great qualities in a man who stood out in society as some-one who could be emulated by grandkids and adults alike. Some people wonder if Albert Einstein could ever make a basket or hit a home run.

Role models are not always made; they evolve. Those special individuals may come to realize they have an influence on the lives of young people. But setting out to be a role model on purpose is usually not the norm. Once he recognizes his elevated place in society, great efforts are usually made to maintain that reputation. This is especially common among professional athletes.

Another role model who was influential in the lives of hundreds of young athletes was Ron Jackson. Jackson drove a bread truck for a living. In his younger days, a couple things happened that developed him into a role model that would be difficult to match. He was a scholar. He received several scholarship offers to study at major colleges and universities. The offers were based on both his scholastics and his ability to play baseball. Like many young athletes, he wanted to pursue a career playing professional baseball. He was well on his way to the Major Leagues when the Korean Conflict began. Just a step away from having his dream come true, he enlisted in the US Army instead. He told people it was his duty as an American citizen to serve his country in the military. Later, according to his wife and family, he probably could have become exempt. But he evaluated his priorities and left his passion for playing baseball in order to serve his country. He played baseball in the military with much success. After an honorable discharge from the Army, his window for playing professional baseball narrowed. He had a family that was more important to him. So he coached and played amateur baseball and softball for years.

His example encouraged others. But here was what made Ron Jackson a special role model. He continued his passion for baseball, teaching young kids. He not only coached baseball for years on almost every level, but he used his opportunity to influence young boys to become men. Almost everything he did on the baseball diamond pointed toward life lessons. Successful men in his community and around the world often claimed that Ron Jackson was their role model.

Grandpa, again, people are watching. Now is the best opportunity ever to strengthen yourself as a role model or establish being one with your grandkids. It's worth it, and it may be something that those grandkids will pass on to their grandkids.

Potential

Grandpa always said that reaching your highest potential is a moving target.

Discovering your capabilities and what you can do with them is one of those things that can make life better. It can challenge you, it sometimes drives you to be more creative and hardworking, and it can cement relationships and give you purpose and a more meaningful life.

The moving target is a pathway for you to follow in attempting to discover your desires and capabilities. The target may send you to another state away from home and friends. It may cause debt in your life as you enroll in a major university or trade school. The target may adjust your thinking and goals.

Grandpa told his family about his trek to discovering his potential in getting an education. He almost flunked out of high school. He had to take a special correspondence course to graduate. All he wanted to do was join the Army and make it a career. Then the target moved. The Army recruiter said his field of interest was not open for training. So Grandpa, in order to avoid the military draft (Vietnam was in full force), enrolled at the local community college and found a job that paid enough to get by. The job was reporting for a local newspaper. The target moved. He enrolled in classes at the local state college and liked it. He studied journalism and set out to find his potential. He worked at a job with the college's sports publicity office and loved it. The target moved again. He felt called into ministry and went to graduate school at the seminary in another state. With a Master's Degree in hand, he pastored a church and traveled, teaching and preaching.

And once again, the target moved. He began work on his doctor's degree in theology and graduated.

The point is, Grandpa followed a moving target because he had a passion to get the highest education he could obtain.

He told his family, "It doesn't have to be about education. You can be the best garbage truck driver in the city. Become the best mechanic you can be. The best house builder. The best dentist."

Finding your potential can help make a better life for you. It doesn't always have to be about money. It could be about supporting a cause. It may involve something other than a career.

How is it done? Grandpa said he wasn't quite sure. The journey to discovery is different for each individual. But he did ask his grandkids, "How would you do it?"

Mints

Grandpa, when any person, a stranger or a friend, does something for you, give him a mint and say, "Good job!"

Every opportunity you find to give out a mint, let that person know he or she has done a good job. People like to hear those words. Whether they are a store clerk, a dump truck driver, a policeman, or a doctor, they like to know they are appreciated for what they do. Don't exclude anyone. It could be the janitor, the produce man at the grocery store, the receptionist, or the drive-through money collector. You can almost be assured that the recipient will grin or giggle when they get their mint.

Keep a pocketful of Wint-O-Green Life Savers. Wint-O-Green seems to be the best-liked mint on earth.

Now, be careful and make sure to hand them out correctly. Do not just hand a mint to anyone and say, "Have a good day." No, sir. There is nothing special about that. Arguably, "Have a good day!" is a stale, worn-out, and overused phrase anyway. Wait until the person is finished with the service, pause and look at them, and then hand them a mint while letting them know they did a good job.

Grandpa gave a mint to a clerk at the store once, and she refused it. That's okay. When they say no, make sure to let them know they did a good job anyway. It's the same with those who ask, "So you think I have bad breath?"

And you remind them again, "Not at all. You did a great job!" Either way, they both smile or laugh. Somebody has brightened up their day.

Time In The Garden

Grandpa, look at the science. You reap what you sow. You can't grow a pear tree from a peanut bush. And carrots do not come from apple trees. So let your grandkids know that what they plant in their minds will produce either certain good thoughts or weeds. It all depends on how they cultivate their mind.

Planting seeds in their minds is like planting them in a garden. If they plant good thoughts in their minds and cultivate them and nurture them with other good thoughts, they will sprout into a strong and positive mind with healthy habits that will be a part of who you are. Good thoughts in, good thoughts out.

In a real garden at home, when you plant good seeds, they grow into good, ripe, and healthy produce or beautiful flowers. You can enjoy the end product because you took the time to care for them and cultivate them.

But in both cases, in their minds and in their gardens, beware of the weeds. Even when good seeds are planted, the weeds appear and attempt to destroy them, choking them off and making them incapable of producing good plants.

Guard your grandkids. Let them know that whatever they put in their minds will show up in their speech and actions. Those weeds in their mind will choke off common sense, and soon, they may render the planter (your grandkids) incapable of making right decisions that will enhance their lives. The weeds grow until making wrong decisions dominate their personality and who you are. If the weeds are not removed from their vegetable garden, the tomatoes and the carrots get choked off and cannot grow to be healthy. So it is with your grandkids if they continually feed their minds with weeds instead of healthy thoughts.

The weeds will choke off the ability to make good decisions, and they will strangle their ability to think clearly and act positively.

"How do we do that, Grandpa?"

Tell them to choose what goes in their brains. Do not allow evil thoughts to creep into your mind. Thoughts like harming people, breaking the law, having nasty thoughts of women or men, and having unhealthy conversations with other people. Refuse to think about those kinds of things. Those are all unhealthy seeds that produce weeds in your mind. They must be removed or not planted in the first place. Removing them takes clear thinking. It takes making good choices. Removing the weeds of your mind means dismissing them and replacing them with good, positive thoughts. It takes concentration.

One way to remove the weeds of your mind is to hang out with other people who are like-minded. The I-used-to-do-that people are those who have conquered bad thoughts that dominated their thinking. Make friends with the people who do things right, like obeying the law, honoring their parents, and being polite to women and men. They are the people who have decided that good seeds of thought that are cultivated are much better than growing weeds in their minds.

Covenant

There was a time when a man's word was his bond. Business was done on a handshake. Lawyers were not needed because the agreements were strong and honest. Grandpa, consider sharing with your grandkids the importance of keeping their word and doing what they say they will do.

It's called a covenant, and under the law, it is a legal document that cannot be broken without consequences. When a covenant is established, it is meant to be honored. It is to be honored with one's word.

The covenant may be written on paper for the purpose of examining its contents, and then it is signed to fulfill the requirements of the law. But it is carried out with the trust and honor of the parties that signed it. The agreement to perform reveals the character of the parties who signed. It says who they are.

To demonstrate keeping your promise is a very important step in shaping a trusting and honorable life. Keeping your word builds and strengthens character and relationships.

Grandpa made a promise that he would take his only grandson to the zoo on Saturday. Saturday came, and so did the rain. It rained so hard many of the roads were closed down. He thought about canceling the zoo trip for obvious reasons. But he remembered what he was sharing with his grandson about keeping his word. Honoring his word was who Grandpa was, and nothing could deter him from keeping his promise.

It didn't matter that both the adventuresome guys nearly drowned in the pouring rain. They were soaked to the skin. They might have been the only visitors at the zoo that day. Even the animals cowered in their caves to avoid the downpour. The point is they were there, period. Grandpa kept his word.

God never broke a promise. He always kept His word. And this is a good opportunity to remind the grandkids that He set the example, and we need to follow it.

"That was a cool trip, Grandpa. I'm freezing, and my tennis shoes are sloshing. I think we should celebrate and reward ourselves with a steaming cup of hot chocolate!"

What a precious lesson was learned by his grandson. And of course, Grandpa had to buy the hot chocolate, again.

Nobody's Perfect

It's good when Grandpas admit they made a mistake. They might just look at their grandkids and confess that they did or said something wrong or hurtful. The mistake probably is not as important as admitting it and apologizing for it. As a Grandpa, your honesty and openness, along with boldness to admit your mistake, is very important. Especially if you approach the job of helping your grandkids become good citizens and fine adults. Being a Grandpa with humility and honesty can set a tremendous example for your grandkids.

Not all Grandpas are perfect. As a matter of fact, there are no perfect Grandpas! Our credibility is based on our honesty. So we should keep it at the forefront of our lives as an example to our grandkids and everyone else. We are fallible, and we miss the mark sometimes. It's not easy to share or admit our weaknesses. In fact, there are people (Grandpas or not) who will probably never admit they are wrong or that they made a mistake. By admitting our flaws, we can build our relationship with our grandkids and increase our credibility.

Now, what impact does that have on being a Grandpa, in particular?

If your grandkids have placed you on a pedestal, your failure to fess up to your wrongdoing may cause that footstool to shake a little. There are grandkids who think their Grandpa can do no wrong. So by showing your grandkids that you are willing to apologize and make things right can positively impact them.

Grandkids can tell when their Grandpa is insincere or faking it. So admitting your mistakes is a way of highlighting your character. It shows that you have integrity. You should own up to your actions. You should be concerned about getting it right the next time. You should be contrite and not boast about it. It's one of those good lessons your grandkids can learn by witnessing your example.

GRANDPA'S WORK ETHIC

Participation Awards

Grandpa, one of the newest and soon-to-be-forgotten practices in the life our grandkids is the participation awards. It's relatively new because of our recent progressive sports psychology, which has been developed to include everybody who takes part in any competitive program. The idea is to give everyone the same award no matter what part they played on the team or if they played at all.

The award is on its way out, thanks to the protests of some coaches, parents, and a lot of Grandpas. The objection to the presentation is that kids need to learn what it means to earn something, especially in competitive events. The system includes even bench sitters getting a trophy. One team in the Mid East gave out trophies to kids that registered but never showed up for games or practice.

One of the lessons here is to encourage young competitors to compete. What the kids do not understand is that there is value in competing as a practice player even if they do not play in the game. Not everyone can make touchdowns, hit home runs, swim faster than the next guy, or win even a chess match. At practice, kids are challenged to develop their interest in the game. If they do not show up for practice or do not come to the games, there should be no awards for just signing up.

Now, Grandpa, how do you encourage your grandkids to learn the value of being a part of the team, no matter what role they may play? One way, and this is at the top of the list, is for you to show up at practice. Better yet, take your grandkid to practice. Let him know that teams practice for a reason. Not everybody can be a superstar. But there is value in an athlete in putting on the equipment and catching batting practice or shagging fly balls. When the team gets better, they do so because practice consisted of everyone taking part.

Next, go to every game and marvel at your grandkid sitting on the bench, picking up bats, or coaching a base. Sit in anticipation of him going into the game when the winning or losing score is out of reach. Cheer him on. Talk it up after the game. Be in the stands so he can see you.

Yes, he may express some disappointment at not being in the starting lineup or not playing very much. But remind him that he is a valuable part of the team. Tell him Johnny would have never hit that home run if you had not been there to help at batting practice.

Participation awards are not bad if they are earned. Perhaps the coach and players together could devise a point system for coming to practice or playing a certain number of innings or quarters. Or playing in the chess competition or swimming at practice and in a swim meet. Whatever the event, they need to actually participate. And let's give serious consideration to changing the name of the award to Value Trophy or Development Award.

Finally, one great baseball coach spent years working with athletes. Many of them sat on the bench more than they played. But in the end, his ball players admitted, along with all the fans and parents, that this man was not really coaching baseball. He was teaching young boys to become men by encouraging them to be a part of the team in every possible way. He once said, "Winning is fun, but it takes work. We play the way we practice, so we work at practice and together we win!" (the late Ron Jackson, former professional baseball player and American Legion Baseball Coach)

Yard Work

Beware, grandkids, your Grandpa will tell you he has a shovel that will fit your hand perfectly. It's a myth. It's not true. They don't make custom shovels to fit hands. It's just a ploy to get you to do yard work.

But don't be misled. Yard work can be a time of fun, bonding, learning, and fellowship. If it's done correctly, Grandpa can actually grow kids and plant flowers at the same time.

As the story goes, Grandpa and the boys were digging in the yard. The grandkids wanted to impress him, so they began at a fast pace and kept it up. But every hour, Grandpa would suggest a break. The boys would forego the rest time and keep on digging. Sometimes they would dig all the harder. Break after break, the young ones kept scooping the dirt. Grandpa stayed loyal to the time schedule and took his break every hour. At the end of the day, his ditch was always deeper and longer. The boys were awestruck. How did he get all that work done and still have the breaks?

"Well," he said, "on every break, I would go to the shed and sharpen my shovel. That way I could dig more dirt with less work."

Learning to do yard work can involve safety as well. Make sure your grandkids know and understand some of the hazards found in a normal yard. As they become smart workers, remind them to pay attention to the details. Before they start doing some serious digging, walk them around the yard and show them where the sprinkler heads and water lines are located. Make sure they are aware of the exact location of underground electrical lines and television cables. If you have a telephone landline, the phone wires need to be located and marked.

Knowing the difference between a weed and one of Grandma's prized flowers is an easy one to master. Details also include using the right tool for the job. It is much easier leveling gravel with a garden rake than a yard rake.

Telling your grandkids about the custom-made shovel hoax is really a way to get them to work within the yard. Next time, you have to come up with something else. So, grandkids, beware when your Grandpa tells you how much fun working a jackhammer can be or how digging up worms in the garden is the best place to find fishing bait.

Trust: Working Unsupervised

Trust is accumulated. It is earned. It takes work to develop and includes a certain amount of camaraderie. When trusting your grandkids to work unsupervised, make sure their age is taken into account. Younger kids need to be shown over and over again how to do the job. They need to demonstrate they have learned what you have taught them. They need assurance that they can be trusted to work alone. If the bond of trust with younger grandkids is broken, then it may take an extra effort to further develop it.

If the grandkids are older, say teenagers, trust is earned. The incentive for the bond of trust is usually money. Eventually, the bond will grow and tighten as you and your grandkids are confident in knowing you can trust each other no matter what.

Teach them to work independently and without supervision. For instance, take cleaning the hot tub. Your teenage grandkids could not be found this Saturday, so you settled for your younger grandkids and enlisted them for the job.

First, ten-year-olds should never be given the job without Grandpa or somebody being there to make sure it's done properly. No-Scrub cleaner should list in the instructions found on the back of the bottle to keep the product out of the hands of ten-year-old grandkids.

So to give a full bottle of No-Scrub cleaner to two ten-year-old grandkids and leave them alone to clean the hot tub is Grandpa's unbelievable mistake. All he wanted to do was help them to make a little money. Wrong. And the price for that kind of mistake is usually high.

Begin with a group hug and explain to them that more is not better. Just a dab of No-Scrub cleaner is plenty. Show them the evidence of how shiny the hot tub is with a single dab. Practice with them to make sure they know and understand the technique.

Then never leave them alone. But you did, thinking you could trust them. After all, you did practice. Note: The furthest thing from their ten-year-old minds was learning to be trusted. They had a full bottle of No-Scrub cleaner, and they were alone.

When Grandpa returned home, the entire spa was hazed over. It was white, with a thick film of gritty chalk-like paste. Every inch of the tub was dulled, and some areas even accumulated what appeared to be spoonfuls of the rubbing compound.

"Well, Grandpa, how do you like it?" they asked with grins on their faces. "We really sweated on it!"

It was difficult for you to tell them they did a good job. They did not do a good job. So what do you do? You couldn't reprimand them and yell at them. You couldn't get mad. You could call the spa store and ask what would be the best way to remove the cleaner, and you explained the situation. It didn't help your disposition to hear the salesman explain that hot tubs were made to never need scrubbing. They had a permanent shine on them. You might begin to boil. Then you realized that these were just ten-year-old kids. Taking a deep breath and counting to 431 might help you calm down.

So you made a quick decision. You told them they needed to sharpen up their job before Grandma got home, and you volunteered to help them. You jumped in the tub with them and started to wipe the No-Scrub cleaner off. About an hour of hard work combined with treating yourself to another cooling-off period and the hot tub looked like it just came off the showroom floor.

Grandma walked out on the deck, smiled, and said, "They sure did a great job. Those little fellas sure can work. Oh, by the way, I already paid them before I went shopping!"

Packing Logs

Grandpa, never underestimate your grandkids.

Here is the scene on a cold winter morning: Two old Grandpas and a borrowed grandkid readied themselves to take on a field full of fallen timber that needed to be cut into rounds, loaded, and delivered. Only one of them was the teacher of the day. He could hardly wait to get out of the truck and pull on his work gloves. He was the leader. Yep, it was the grandkid.

Although he was a rookie in the lumber business, he had learned the value of hard work from his Grandpa and his father. And did he ever learn it well. The old guys were amazed at his enthusiasm and his wisdom. Many of his predecessors who had been hired to do a job had a history of becoming tired and quitting early. From the beginning, the Grandpas knew there was no doubt this job would be finished ahead of time.

The other two workers, both in their seventies, had years of experience under their belts and stood ready to get the job done. Most of the logs were already cut and lying on the ground. They all decided that the first task would be to load the trailer. The Grandpas were quite satisfied with just tossing them in. After all, they were going to be unloaded in less than an hour. With a dozen logs in the trailer, they watched as the grandkid stepped back, evaluated the situation, laid down his log, and began sorting and stacking the wood in the trailer. He said he hoped that it was all right to do it that way, explaining to the Grandpas that the trailer could carry more wood if they stacked it neatly instead of just tossing it in. Brilliant.

Meanwhile, the Grandpa with the chainsaw kept the wood toters busy. With the grandkid loading the trailer, the other Grandpa took charge of loading the pickup.

Somehow, he complained that the logs seemed heavier than last time. Instead of tossing pieces of trees in the back of the truck, he cradled each one like he was carrying a baby and placed it down gently in the bed. The grandkid was tossing logs twice the size in the trailer while stacking them on every fourth or fifth toss. What should have been an example of good work management being taught by the Grandpas turned into them staring in disbelief at the youngster working like a machine.

Now, remember there was a bridge of about sixty years in age between him and each of the Grandpas. The respect the boy had for older folks was amazing. He took the heavy ones and left the kindling sticks and smaller logs for them.

The Grandpa with the chainsaw, however, laid it aside and jumped in. It was hard to tell if it was his goal to keep up with the grandkid or not. But he did. So on the way to delivering the wood, it was decided that the Grandpa with the chainsaw had cut and stacked more wood than both of them put together, and he had been doing it for years. He was in pretty good shape.

At the delivery point, the grandkid didn't make a decision as to where the wood was going to be stacked until Mom gave the directions. Then the show was on again. This time, the grandkid jumped on top of the stacked wood and turned his back to the trailer's downed tailgate and began kicking each piece of wood in the direction of the designated pile. Old Grandpa slowly took each piece from the pickup and tossed it in the pile. His body was aching in places he didn't know he had places. The kid never even slowed down.

It took about an hour to load all the logs and just eighteen minutes to unload and stack them. As Grandpa stood, catching his breath, the grandkid grabbed a snow shovel and began tossing out all the bark. It was needed for kindling, he explained.

Grandpa said he knew that.

All in all, it was a delightful work party. It just seemed normal to the young eager beaver. The big difference in this party was that instead of the Grandpas teaching the grandkid, it was the other way around. And that was not all.

As the pickup was preparing to pull out of the driveway and the two workers shook hands, Grandpa said he would see about renting a wood splitter so they could split and stack the wood for better drying.

"No, that's okay," the grandkid said with a kind and gentle voice (he wasn't even out of breath). "I always wanted to get an ax and learn to split wood!"

Value Of Hard Work

Grandpa, one of the most valuable gifts in life that you can give to your grandkids is to teach them the value of hard work.

Playing video games all day, spending most of the day perfecting an ollie on the skateboard, and wearing out a cell phone keyboard texting half the school won't pay the rent.

Hard work is not strictly laboring at a task. It includes using your brain as well as your body. In other words, physically working at a job is one thing. But hard work means knowing how to work smart. Have the right tools for the job, plan out the task, and attack the project with the attitude of completing it in a reasonable amount of time. You may remind your grandkids that that doesn't come in one or two easy lessons. It takes trial and error, practice, and an awareness of what other workers are doing around them.

Teaching work values includes having something for your grandkids to do when they visit. Washing and waxing the car is hard work, but it's only done once or twice a year in the summertime. Pulling weeds and hoeing the garden are hard work, but the reward is a good-looking yard and a healthy garden or lawn. It takes time, and grandkids should learn that a small job cannot take half the day to complete. Pay them well so they develop an eagerness to work and earn money.

Even though our modern technology offers an automatic dishwasher, grandkids should know how to wash dishes. Automatic dishwashers break down from time to time. The dishes still need to be cleaned and dried and put away. Teach them why the table needs to be cleared after a meal. And there is a proper way to set the table and serve the meal. You may be careful not to make every visit to your house a lesson in hard work. If that becomes the case, soon, the grandkids may rather skateboard, play videos, or sleep instead of visiting you.

Grandpa and Grandma can team up and teach grandkids how to do their own laundry. If a young girl or boy can learn how to do laundry properly, a lot of money is ready to be made at college. It's cheaper for fellow students to pay somebody to do their laundry than to pay for gas to drive home and have it done. Most college kids may admit they do not like doing laundry.

One Grandpa taught his grandson how to cut hair. He was licensed by the state when he reached the proper age and made lots of money at college barbering. It was hard work, and he needed to juggle his time so his studying did not suffer.

Grandma taught her grandson how to iron clothes. Even with college kids wearing nonwrinkling clothes, some students prefer the neat, nonwrinkled look. Ironing a dress shirt is a skill. A simple idea turned into earning lots of money.

The value of hard work should be integrated into your grandkid's thinking. It is a skill, a habit, and an attitude all rolled into one that will help build a road to the future in all areas of life. Hard workers are able to take on more responsibility because they know how to work smart and balance their time. It helps them prioritize and organize their lives.

Grandpa, teaching your grandkids the value of hard work is a gift to them. It is a gift that increases in value as life goes on. There are so many rewards for those who value hard work. It is also a gift that can be passed on to your great-grandkids as well. What a blessing it is to be a part of that.

No Reward Grades

Grandpa, when grandkids get their report cards, their learning does not end. For a good reason, you may reconsider not giving them a reward with money, cars, prizes, or trips.

It is important that grandkids understand the value of learning for the sake of learning. Report cards and grades are simply an indication of their learning experience and their progress. The goal is misguided when the final grades on the report card are the most important thing. Your grandkids should be taught and inspired to always do their best. Final grades should be challenging. If the card reads straight As or contain average grades, the challenge should be maintaining the perfect scores or working hard to improve the other marks.

Rewards are good. Who would deny that? Grandkids love them. But there is a danger worth avoiding. Offering rewards that are expensive or luxurious can misguide the purpose of education.

Your grandkids actually begin working when they enter the first grade, in that going to school and studying is their job. Recognition for work that is well done should not be denied. Adults may receive accolades in their workplace for doing their job well. They may even receive a bonus. In the Army, they call it pro-pay, which means the soldiers are doing extremely hazardous jobs, like jumping out of airplanes or fighting in a war.

Rewards for the sake of rewards can be draining and costly. There are some students who have received a car or a trip to Europe for earning good grades.

Grandpas can lead the way by encouraging their grandkids to excel in school. And a treat, such as a Blizzard or a special dinner, should suffice. It spotlights them, pumps them up, and encourages them.

In days past, Grandma would put on a pot of beans, bake a pan of cornbread, and cook some collard greens when the grandkids brought home their report cards. It wasn't the meal. It was the celebrating that counted.

And by the way, that was some fine dining.

Inventing Things To Do

Grandpa, if your grandkids are willing to work and are having a difficult time finding a job, help them invent one.

Not many careers are made dog walking, but the latest rumor is that it pays well if it is done correctly. Like most unique jobs, the idea of convincing the customers to pay somebody to walk their dogs is the difficult part. Let your grandkid know that walking the dog is a service that must be sold. It's stressful to the dog owner when the health of the dog is at stake. The grandkid must convince him that his walking distance and pace is best for his pooch. Treat it like any other business, and work hard to make it grow. For instance, walk more than one dog at the same time. You are limited only by your imagination.

People also pay to have fresh vegetables delivered to their door. And grocery store managers would rather pay less money to have the same products delivered by a young entrepreneur directly from the farm. Farmers will allow self-harvesting and bagging of their products in order to save money. And the money your grandkid makes can be substantial if he works at it.

Creating a business that delivers birthday and special occasion cakes on the college campus can produce money. How convenient is it for Mom and Dad to order a special cake for their college kid and then have it delivered right to their dormitory door? There are some logistics involved, and your grandkid will have to make an initial investment, but an ingenious college kid can make some money at it. Where else can you find a custom-made you-aced-the-course or a thanks-for-the-touchdown-we-won cake for under five bucks? Cakes can be mass-produced in small, individual-sized cake tins. He can make a dozen cakes for less than twenty dollars in ingredients. Every dormitory has a stove and oven in the social area. Bake late at night. Local thrift stores have used baking pans for sale. Run off some flyers for advertising and post them on and around the campus. Let the students send them home to Mom and Dad or aunts and uncles. There are several ways to make this work if your grandkid is willing to tackle it.

One more idea: buy and bag your own refreshments for sporting events. A fifty-pound bag of salted in-the-shell peanuts doesn't cost that much. Buy lunch bags in bulk. Sunflower seeds and candy in bulk can be found at the cash-and-carry outlet. Encourage your grandkids to work and let them discover the joy of making trips to the bank every Monday. And enjoy being your grandkid's personal consultant.

Hobbies

Grandpa, there are a ton of reasons why you should encourage your grandkids to learn a skill outside their projected profession. It's called a hobby.

Young grandkids may not have experienced it yet, but the world is full of stress. There are fewer and fewer places to relax. Eventually, your grandkids may learn that the pressure of finding a job in their chosen field or learning to become an expert in that field is not the most relaxing journey in the world.

So here is an opportunity for you to be a great encouragement to them. Help them learn to relax by prompting them to do something completely outside of their comfort zone. Challenge them to explore (in fact, explore with them) skills, crafts, and activities that will take them away from the rat race. Try to avoid making their goal earning money. If money is the goal of learning to do something relaxing, it may soon become a second profession or side job, which may add stress as they labor to pay for it or add tension as they work to improve the product.

Let's look at a few examples by way of mentioning people who took Grandpa at his word and created hobbies outside their professions.

One Grandpa, when he was a young mortician or funeral director, learned to be a skilled leather craftsman. He could make almost anything out of leather. He even attempted to make a leather suit for a man. He was successful, and his hobby took him away from the stress of the day.

There was a Grandpa who could whistle like a bird. He was in a local whistling club that traveled to competitions. They performed at social events and weddings, birthday parties, and even a funeral or two. Practice was a time to talk about whistling and to learn new songs and techniques.

This Grandpa was a brain surgeon by profession. One of the whistlers spent time with another performance club in town—a ukulele orchestra. The musical troupe performed whenever they could find a place to play. When he wasn't whistling or strumming his ukulele, he was the local Dog Catcher.

Encouraging your grandkids to learn to do something new gives you an opportunity to either learn with them, cheer them on, or help them buy materials, which would make you part of the experience.

Here are a few more ideas just for fun. A friend who worked in construction operating a jackhammer all day spent many hours after work painting the inside of eggs. Watching it was amazing. First, he had to empty the egg without breaking the shell. Then he had to get the right lighting on the shell and get a paintbrush small enough to fit in a small hole. It was fascinating. He actually had to paint backward.

Then there were the two professional football players carrying a combined weight of over six hundred pounds and looking mean. You know what they did at work. They hurt people. One of them shed his pads and did needlework. Not knitting or crocheting, but with the tiny little thread used for tatting. He made fine lace with his two gigantic hands and fingers. The other defensive tackle headed for the dance studio to learn ballet and tap dance. He realized he probably could not make this a lifelong hobby, so he worked at learning choreography. He wrote dances. Then he performed his original work with the other dancers at recitals and local talent shows.

Grandpa, once again, you and your grandkids are limited only by your imagination and what leads you to uniqueness. Be a friend to your grandkids. Help them discover a few things that could spark them to develop another side of themselves.

GRANDPA'S STORIES

Grandpa And The Cow

Okay, I admit I'm a city slicker. I don't like cows, and horses scare me. I don't get along with goats or ducks or chickens. They are not my favorite farm animals.

There is a reason for that. Cows don't like me, horses have lots of friends and don't need any more, and goats are not real animals. Ducks and chickens attack me and peck me.

So why are we mentioning this bit of tomfoolery? Grandkids love to hear their Grandpa tell stories about himself. Especially if they get better as the years go on.

When Grandma and I were young, we rented a five-acre farm with two barns and a corral. We didn't have any animals, but the neighbors did. It was sort of a share-the-land situation. Anyway, why would I get animals on purpose? They had three cows and some chickens. I had a new pair of cowboy boots and a Western jacket. I wanted to play the part. Almost every night, I would watch my neighbor bring in the cows. It was a simple job and looked like it could be fun. After all, how dangerous could it be leading a cow to the barn?

So I mustered up all the courage I needed and buttoned up my jacket. After slipping on my new leather gloves, I straightened my borrowed cowboy hat and moved out toward the cow. I was ready to be the conqueror. I needed the bragging rights of telling the adventurous story of how I led a mean bull back to the barn for milking.

Focused on the size of this mighty beast, our eyes met as I stepped right in the middle of a fresh cow pie with my brand-new cowboy boots. I didn't know what to do. The cow was looking at me, and the neighbor was laughing. Maybe the cow was laughing too. I had no idea what a laughing cow sounded like, so I just assumed it was him. Instantly, I did what I thought was the most logical thing; I jumped onto the fence to prevent the cow from charging me, just like a real cowboy. Of course, getting away from the cow was done for my own safety.

With the cow under control, the neighbor handed me the lead rope and a coffee can half full of grain. He said all I had to do was extend the rope and shake the can lightly, and the cow would follow me. Okay, I took the can and sort of ambled out ahead of the cow. I started shaking the can like it was a set of castanets. I would be lying if I said I was not a little scared. The cow just plodded along. At this point, I just wanted to get it over with, so I walked a little faster. The cow saw this and began to speed up. He wasn't running, mind you, but he was focused.

I thought for a minute the cow was getting too involved in my feeding technique, so I began to jog. So did the cow.

"Drop the can, drop the can!" my friend yelled.

As I let go of the can, I stumbled over my own feet but didn't fall down. New cowboy boots are very difficult to run in. Here came the cow, charging at what could have been full speed. At the time, it looked like his head was down and smoke was streaming from his nose and ears. He was charging with a purpose. I could see it in his eyes. It was very obvious to me at this point that the cow did not like me, and there was no way we could ever be friends. My borrowed cowboy hat went flying, and I fell to the ground. I covered my head with my arms as I rolled up in a ball. That cow wanted to kill me.

When I looked up, there he was, nosing the can and chomping on the grain. Thinking that I might have had the beginning of a heart attack would be a little melodramatic. But the old ticker was working overtime. My neighbor rescued me and grabbed the lead rope. He didn't say anything as he led the cow to the barn.

I still don't socialize with cows, chickens, goats, or ducks. Sitting in my uptown condominium sipping a latte is more to my liking.

Having survived this farm adventure, I now consider myself to be a certified city slicker. And I really do admire cowboys who dodge mean bulls all day and then struggle at night to pull them into the barn for milking. It's just not my cup of tea.

Cooking A Carp

"Grandpa, Uncle Jimmy said he was going fishing next week, and he hopes he catches a carp. What is a carp?"

A carp is what they call a "bottom fish." That means they eat stuff on the bottom of the lake or pond. Usually, what they eat is not too pleasant, so when you catch a carp, it won't taste very good, and it will be very bony. Some people say that if you cook a carp correctly, it may taste pretty good. Others won't eat a carp, but they like to fish for them because they put up such a rousing fight.

"How do you cook a carp, Grandpa?"

"Well," began Grandpa, "it's kind of a specialty, and people use different methods."

When you bring the carp home, you make sure it is cleaned well. Soaking it in hot water will take off as much of the outer layer as possible. It improves the cooking time and makes the preparation easier. Then you fillet it and put it on a pine board. This enhances the flavor while it is in the oven. The best way is to smear butter all over it from head to tail.

"You mean you leave the head on it?"

"Yessir, my boy! There's something about leaving the head on the fish that makes the whole experience seem native. Then you drizzle olive oil all over the carp, add salt and pepper, and let it set for eleven minutes. Meanwhile, heat up the oven to about 350 degrees."

The next thing is really special. It's called the magic ingredient. You add garlic. Garlic adds flavor to any fish, but it's magic the way it transforms the flavor of a carp. Before placing it in the oven, wrap it in tin foil and squeeze a lemon and a lime all over it and let it sit for three more minutes. Make sure it sets for only three minutes. Any longer and the meat begins to separate. After three minutes, take the tin foil off and place it on the pine board. This is what separates the real chef from the amateur chef. Use fish tongs to lift it out of the tin foil. If you move it with your fingers, the strength of the garlic will be weakened because the garlic is disturbed. Do not let your fingers touch the fish at this point.

Now place the pine board with the fish on it in the oven for nine and a half minutes. Remember, nine and a half minutes. Not ten minutes, but nine and a half. When the buzzer goes off, you carefully open the oven. If you open the oven too fast, the fish may begin to fall apart, so you have to be slow and careful.

Take out the pine board, throw the fish in the garbage, and eat the pine board. Then you nudge your grandkid on the shoulder and say, "I'm just messing with you!"

The Story

Grandpas like to tell stories. In fact, many Grandpas are famous for telling too many stories. For this Grandpa, each one of his stories was unique. It was fun just listening to the inflection in his voice. When he came to an exciting part, he would stop for a minute and rub his chin. The grandkids knew what was next. He would move to the edge of his chair while planting his feet solidly on the floor. Then, like a crocodile getting ready to attack his prey, he would stand up real fast, raise his eyebrows, and make his point. The only thing was his point did not have any resemblance to the drama of a hungry crocodile. It was just his way of getting everyone excited. But the grandkids laughed and egged him on.

Sometimes his grandkids were not in the mood for a story, but they could almost count on Grandpa offering one. The key was not to catch his eye. Whenever somebody caught his eye, out came the story, like it or not. The grandkids used to sneak around the house when Grandpa was home. He would be sitting in his favorite chair, reading the newspaper, and pretending he didn't hear them.

"Don't look him in the eye," they whispered. Examining his every move like a sentry, they hoped he wouldn't lower the paper and catch somebody's eye. Almost like clockwork, the paper came crashing down, and Grandpa whipped off his reading glasses.

The grandkids looked away so fast you would think they saw the wicked witch of the house. They ran and scattered like a bevy of quail being discovered by a fox.

Grandpa just smiled and went back to his paper.

The grandkids peeked around the corner and giggled. It had become a game now. Grandpa peeked back at them until it was obvious somebody lost the attempted stare down. With very little fanfare, he just motioned the kids over to his well-worn leather chair, and he announced he had a new story for them. They were excited. It began, and his new story had never been heard before.

That is, the new beginning of the story had never been heard before.

They were trapped. It was one of the same old stories, only with a new introduction. The grandkids endured the story, as usual, but this time, when Grandpa was finished telling it, they ran to the kitchen for cookies and milk. With their backs turned to Grandpa, they whispered to each other, "Don't look him in the eye, don't look him in the eye!"

GRANDPA'S MEMORIES

Technology

Grandpa, having a great respect for your grandkids when it comes to technology can be to your advantage in more ways than one. When it comes to computers and cell phones, chances are, they know more than the average Grandpa. They can easily perform like well-trained nerds with anything that even resembles a piece of today's technology. The Technology Age may have passed some of us by.

"The first portable telephone I ever used was packed in a suitcase about the size of a french horn," a Grandpa in Washington reported.

"Glorious was the day they disappeared and we welcomed the Brick, a device the size of three bananas tied together. We could talk to somebody three hundred miles away for free, but a call to the backyard to ask Grandma if she needed anything at the grocery store was a long-distance charge." He laughed.

It sure was nice when the Flip Phone made its appearance. One of the difficulties in using this small device was that a big man with flat thumbs and fat fingers could hardly ever produce a readable text message.

As the technology developed rapidly, so did the price of the equipment. Back then, when you purchased a cell phone, it seemed more like an investment. Most of them began at $400.

The salesman said the new Flip Phones were like having a computer in your pocket. Most Grandpas asked, "Why would I want a computer in my pocket when all I want to do is make a plain ole phone call?"

The instruments are so advanced today it is almost unbelievable what they can do. The price has gone up to around $1,200 and so has its capabilities. Some grandkids work those gadgets like they were international businessmen. They can trade on the stock market or create a masterpiece musical composition on their way to school.

Most Grandpas have butt dialing down to an art.

Technology in Grandpa's day was an answering machine, a transistor radio, and car windows that rolled up automatically. When something broke, the fix-it man made as much as two dollars an hour repairing it. Repair work today begins at $104 an hour plus parts. That little computer you carry in your pocket will allow you to watch major movies, talk to almost anyone in the world, fix your plumbing from a distance, build a spare room in your house, or make reservations for flights, hotels, and car rentals with one call. And more. Much more. Just ask your grandkids.

Nowadays, if your computer freezes up or your cell phone refuses to perform, you can call your grandkids to come to the rescue. He or she will probably proceed to push three buttons, hand it to you, and announce that it is ready to go. It would not surprise most Grandpas to learn that their ten-year-old grandkid could hack into the Federal Reserve System on his phone during his lunch break.

Bet you're glad you went to college!

Singing In Church

Grandpa could sing!

Once years ago, he revealed that he sang with the famous Blackwood Brothers Gospel Quartet. It was amazing. He never mentioned that before. It must have been when the group was young and just getting started.

"Yessir, my boy." He grinned with a twinkle in his eye. "I would turn on the tape recorder, jump in the shower, and sing and sing and sing! Bing Crosby and I were good together too!"

Since the first time he told those stories, he admitted he got a lot of mileage out of them.

One of the pleasures of life was sitting in church singing hymns with Grandpa.

He never looked at the book because he knew the words by heart. People in the congregation looked at him and just grinned. He was in his own world. He sang so loud he was always noticed, and the whole church could hear him.

Some people claimed the gas station man and the folks in the sawmill could easily hear him too.

The grin on his face was contagious. It rippled through that small congregation like skipping a rock on a quiet pond.

Grandpa was sitting on the bank of the river fishing when his grandkid said, "Grandpa, I didn't know you were so musical. When did you learn to read music?"

It was almost like walking into a trap. His grandkid could see the answer coming.

"Well, son, I read music by the letter. I just look toward heaven, open my mouth, and let 'er fly!"

He loved taking his gift to church with him. Age had tattered his tuner. It was a little rusty. He said it was everyone else who was off pitch and not him. The comments often were used as a joke, but he seemed to take it graciously.

What a joy it was for him to sit with his family. On one special Sunday, the congregation had extended the music portion of the service. The people were smiling and filled with enthusiasm. After the place settled down, the preacher stood up with his Bible under his arm and shuffled toward the pulpit. He was silent for what seemed a long time.

Then he warmed the hearts of the entire congregation when he said with his most tender voice, "Slick, you help me preach!" Amen, brother, Amen.

Note: Slick is the Grandpa who lived in a log cabin in the woods in the Ozark Mountains.

Just A Nice Story

Let's set the stage for just a neat and meaningful story about Grandpa. Realizing that several others could tell great stories about their Grandpas, this one seemed particularly interesting for a couple reasons. At a men's meeting at the church, cards were passed out to dads with the idea of them giving them to their children. Printed on the cards was "What did you learn from your Grandpa?" And on the back was "What did you teach your Grandpa, and how did you teach him?"

The cards came back with evidence that they were not passed on to children but were filled out by adults. At the meeting were several professional people, including doctors, dentists, a college professor, and a couple retired folks. Following is a story by Dr. Joe (not his real name). It has no particular lesson or moral. It is just a nice story about a guy's Grandpa.

My *tsuy'e* taught me the gentle ways of the Navajo and the proud ways of the Apache. (A *tsuy'e* is a maternal grandfather.) He had the only mercantile store for almost a hundred miles in the land of the White Mountain Apache. He spoke fluent Navajo and Apache like no other *bilayaava* (white man). My mom was born in the back of the store with the help of an Apache midwife. My mom was about six or seven years old when she watched *Alchesay* (the last hereditary Apache tribal chief) ride his horse up to the town church, with their thirty elders, to be baptized. It was a first. The tribal people would never be the same. I learned that tribal children were primarily taught by their maternal Grandpas. After attending white schools and churches, the children were excluded from learning the old ways and traditions. Of course, now tribal council is big business, and the casinos are run by disenfranchised tribal people with law degrees. It almost broke his heart.

Grandma and Grandpa moved to California, and his gentle ways came with him. I never learned all that he could have taught me. It's the Apache way. I still do not knock on doors (Apaches don't do that). I am always greeted with the Apache *ya'at'eeh* (a common greeting). Even after Grandpa had several strokes, his bent wrist and his palm raised meant "hello" in both Navajo and Apache. Grandpa had lost his voice.

As a result of the things I learned and experienced from Grandpa and the tribal nations, I am not a huge fan of big government and megachurches. My Grandpa taught me a way to act that was much better than simply learning the ABCs of tribal traditions. The gentle spirit of Jesus and my Grandpa still lives within me.

The world is filled with stories like this that are inspirational and meaningful. Not all meetings with Grandpa produce super interesting stories. But there are times when we can sit and ask questions and just let Grandpa tell them. It preserves our heritage and inspires us to pass on our own stories to our grandkids.

Kids like to hear stories, so here is your chance, Grandpa.

Grandpa Is As Grandpa Does

Twelve Grandpas met one day, and the discussion centered around grandkids. For most of the questions that were asked, there were twelve different stories. It may not have been entirely conclusive, but it can be safely said that every Grandpa is different.

Where may you fit into the discussion?

The Grandpa's Manual: What have you learned from your grandkids?

Joe: I must say that each one is different. We talk about a lot of stuff, and sometimes, we don't agree, but all my grandkids have an opinion. And that is refreshing.

Sam: I have ten grandkids, mostly teenagers, and they can't agree on anything! Some of them try to set up Grandpa and disagree just to get a rise out of me. But basically, they have verbal battles whenever we meet. That is really fun.

Dan: Most of my grandkids are adults, and they are forever complimenting Grandpa on the things I have taught them. There is a long list of things, and I am such a genius! The list keeps growing.

The Grandpa's Manual: What about Grandma?

Eli: Grandma has been the love of my life, and they know it. More than a half century she has been my sweetheart and my girlfriend. It's not competitive, but Grandma may have a greater influence on our grandkids than me. But that's okay because we talk about the things that matter and our relationship with our grandkids.

And if there is ever a major decision concerning us and them, she usually delivers the message!

David: Grandma died at an early age, and I never remarried. My grandkids do not have memories of her, but they know we were close. And I think they wish they could have known her.

The Grandpa's Manual: What is the craziest thing you ever did with your grandkids?

Sam: We went snipe hunting. If you don't know what snipe hunting is, look it up! My kids gave me a hard time about that one. A couple of the grandkids cried and didn't like it, but we all hugged and laughed, and it was okay. It's one of those once-in-a-lifetime things, that's for sure.

Richard: We went to Six Flags Over Texas for the day and had a great time. Well, almost! After much coercion, I agreed to go on every ride with them. Let me put it this way: Not all grandkids understand that a heart attack or fainting spell could happen to anyone at any time. It was that scary! The recovery time after every ride increased as the day went on. I almost vomited after the roller coaster. I'll have to say it was fun and the craziest thing I ever did! The grandkids were merciless. There wasn't an ounce of sympathy for Grandpa anywhere!

Del: I got a few friends together, and we went frog gigging. In the dark, the grandkids had no idea where we were, and it was a good thing. We were out in the middle of a cow pasture at the watering hole. That's where the frogs are. We made some gigs out of coat hangers and broomsticks by grinding them into spears. I took a few baseball bats with us just in case we missed the frog. Gigging takes some practice if you are going to be good at it. We were up to our hips in whatever is around cow watering holes. We tried to gig twice and were lousy shots. The frogs got away. So we spent the rest of the adventure shining our flashlights in the frogs' eyes and smashing them with a bat. It was a crazy time with my grandkids. I went frog gigging with my Grandpa when I was a kid. That night, we got over a hundred frogs and skinned them, threw away the bodies, and fried up the legs.

The *Grandpa's Manual: Which one of your grandkids do you love the most, if there is one?*

Dave: I learned this from my wife. We love the one who needs it the most at the time!

And all the Grandpas agreed.

GRANDPA'S LIFE

What? I'm A Grandpa?

When he heard that he was going to be a Grandpa, he nearly freaked out.

Admittedly, his image of a Grandpa was a gray-haired man sitting in a rocking chair just waiting for his grand-kids to rush him, spill his coffee, and sit on his lap. It's not much of a surprise that there are still some Grandpas like that. But here he was, fifty years old, deep in his career, all the kids away from home, and God decided to make him a Grandpa.

Stunned at first, he just sat and stared. How would he spend time with babies and toddlers? And then one day, teenagers and young adults? It seemed so overwhelming, and the grandkid had not even been born yet.

Being a Grandpa is important work. You are one whether you like it or not. The question is, What kind of Grandpa are you going to be? You can't refuse the position. It's yours. So perhaps the best thing to do is admit it, accept it, and set out to be the best one you can be.

Some men imagine that there are guidelines for being a Grandpa. That may be true, and you may wonder where they originated. Some are in the Bible, and some are offered by other Grandpas who feel they have mastered the position. For example, just so you know, Solomon tells us that "children's children are the crown of old men; and the glory of children are their fathers" (Proverbs 17:6). Some of the guidelines for being a Grandpa get to be made up. You create your own set of guidelines. Soon you may realize that whatever works is probably the best guide. For instance, Titus, another writer in the Bible, describes the characteristics of men who are or may become Grandpas. He writes, "[Older men] are to be temperate, worthy of respect, self-controlled and sound in faith, in love and in endurance" (Titus 2:2). The challenge of gaining those characteristics could help in determining what kind of Grandpa you may become.

Here are why men should gladly accept their role of being a Grandpa: It is a part of life that is painted with extra joy and surprises. It gives you something to feel a part of and challenges you to take on the responsibility of guiding your grandkids into being all they can be and doing what is important in life.

There is another reason for being a good Grandpa, and it's easy to overlook. Some Grandpas even refuse to accept it. Being a good Grandpa is pleasing to God. Why? He invented Grandpas. There isn't anything to get antsy about just because it is a God thing. When you think about it, it doesn't even have to be a religious thing. That's just the way it is. We cannot deny the fact that Heaven is where Grandpahood was invented, and it came to earth in the form of wailing babies who one day will become your pride and joy.

So the overemotional freaking out will dissipate as you begin to get used to the new title. As time goes on and more and more grandbabies arrive, you will probably start loving your role. The older grandkids will want you to be a more active part of their generation while the younger ones will just want to run and jump and beg you for ice cream. And it will become a joyful challenge in a society that needs well-raised grandkids who know how to respect others, love their fellow man, obey the laws, and contribute to the world in which they live.

Yes, it really is an important job.

Does Age Make A Difference?

Another image of a Grandpa is an old man with gray hair, sometimes with false teeth, and with a head accented with baldness. He may have bifocals and a big belly. It makes for good fodder for a cartoonist, but the image is fading.

Grandpas are younger and seem to be more active nowadays. Instead of Grandpa keeping up with the grandkids, his grandkids have to try keeping up with him.

How do you handle the modern-day grandkids in an advanced society that was once just a dream?

The simple answer is this: the same way Grandpas have done it for ages, through relationships. Relationships with your grandkids are constant. Only the activities change. Moral principles, mortality, discipline, obedience, and love seldom change. So it is important that you and your grandkids establish and maintain a solid relationship of mutual respect and concern for each other.

For example, discipline in the early days might have meant doing extra chores, taking an occasional hickory switch to bare legs, or going to bed early for a week. Nowadays, discipline could mean taking away the cell phone for a few days, not using the car for a couple weekends, or restricting them from the health spa. The law of the land and the laws of Mom and Dad's house hardly ever change. Respect and obedience remain the same, manners are consistent, and hard work to make a living hasn't changed that much.

The traditional image of Grandpa on the farm tugging at the plow behind the mules may have changed. But love for your grandkids and a sincere desire for them to grow up and become strong, contributing adults still is at the head of the list.

Sure, the old fogies may enjoy a rousing game of checkers on the porch with the grandkids while the forty-something Grandpas are zooming down zip lines, fighting the rapids in a raft, and working out at the arcade playing video games. But still, both generations are with their grandkids, enjoying a relationship, learning new ideas, and mutually striving to do the right thing.

Our society shifts activities as the generations pass us by, but some things seem to remain the same. Grandpa loving his grandkids and relating to them in the best possible way is one of those things.

Young Grandpas

The more things change, the more they remain the same.

Take young Grandpas, for instance. They are not necessarily getting younger; it just seems that way. The forty-something generation seems to approach relationships with their grandkids differently than they did with their own Grandpas. It's a sign of the times.

How do young Grandpas relate to their grandkids today? Dozens of young Grandpas expressed their concern and came to the conclusion that the key is relationships. They said Grandpas can do things with their grandkids and send gifts seemingly forever and still not necessarily have a good relationship with them. The value of having a well-developed relationship with your grandkid is the time you spend with each other. As great as it may seem for grandkids, activities and presents cannot take the place of spending time together reading, talking, sharing, and actually getting to know each other.

Genuine relationships of love and caring have no age limit. A Grandpa can be in his eighties or he can be in his forties.

At a meeting of Grandpas, it was concluded that the differing factor in developing a strong relationship might be found in the environment and in the circumstances in which they live. For example, some Grandpas lean toward teaching their grandkids certain principles when they live on a farm. They might use the environment to express the lessons of life. Things like the value of growing your own food and raising animals that will eventually end up on the table. Whereas, a Grandpa who lives in the city might put emphasis on being safe in the city, knowing how to protect oneself, or knowing how to flag down a taxi. So the environment plays a large part in how grandkids relate to their Grandpa and vice versa.

Here is the common ground, they said. No matter what generation your Grandpa lived in, the basic principles of life and growing up are very similar today. Because of the relationship with your grandkids, you probably want them to be healthy, learn to respect authority, be polite, have fun, be adventuresome, and love you back.

The things you teach your grandkids are timeless. They span generations.

Grandpa, some things just don't seem to change that much. Your grandkids need to learn the value of relationships and some basic principles of life. And you can teach them, regardless of your age.

Surrogate Grandpa

I am a surrogate Grandpa. For me, that means I have no children, neither do I have any grandkids of my own, yet three of the nicest kids I have ever met call me Grandpa. For other Grandpas who have been blessed with their own grandkids, it means the kids who call them Grandpa because they have no Grandpa of their own are really bonus grandkids.

Since Grandpa-grandkid relationships are based on love, concern, respect, and a little craziness at times, it is quite common and acceptable for unrelated people to claim the title and play the role of Grandpa. I think that is a good idea.

I started meeting my three grandkids about five years ago as I welcomed them into the world. They live down the street and play in the neighborhood. Their parents and grandma and I attend the same church, so we see each other often. We are good friends. We remember each of them on birthdays and Christmas and other special occasions.

At first, our families had backyard cookouts, went on picnics, and fished together. We just seemed to be a fixture in their family. As each one of the kids grew and could recognize us, the Grandpa-grandkid relationship began, and they picked out names for us. I am Bert (probably for Bert and Ernie on *Sesame Street*), and my wife is Graham Cracker. We have no idea where that came from.

We wanted to make sure it was okay and proper for them to do this. They already have grandparents, so we made sure nobody would be offended.

I have never been a Grandpa before, so I wondered what one was supposed to do. After all, being crowned with a title and endowed with a special relationship must require a list of rules or something. The supposed uniqueness of being a surrogate Grandpa is not unique at all. I get to be like a real Grandpa and just be myself. Of course, it seems that by nature, Grandpas should pass on wisdom and principles of life, tell stories, and get a little crazy sometimes. One thing I had to be sensitive about was to make sure I never usurped their parents and always kept open lines of communication with them. After all, I am not their parent, and certain things in life that are parental should leave Grandpa out of it. That makes sense, and I agree.

My experience as a surrogate Grandpa has been a wonderful journey. My grandkids are getting older and are encountering some growing pains. Most of their situations are healed by the support and love of their parents. They are wonderful parents and are allowing their kids to take responsibilities as they mature. With that comes a growing relationship with their Grandpa. So we just talk whenever we can. Sometimes we talk at length as they seek advice and share some of their life situations, which may create a need for healing. I also like that part of being a Grandpa. I see too many Grandpas playing the role of jolly old men, always laughing and clowning around and nothing more. Their relationships are often shallow.

Surrogate Grandpas are not ceremoniously created. They evolve out of friendship, love, and respect. My experience has greatly enriched my life, and I think my grandkids feel the same way.

Do What You Want To Do

Grandpa, the old adage goes something like this: "If it's not immoral, illegal, or fattening, you do what you want to do."

Some people believe that because you are getting up in years that you deserve to be able to do whatever you want to do. Others may say you have earned the right to do whatever you want to do. That advice is mythical.

After hours of interviews, we have come to learn that several Grandpas do whatever they want to for a variety of reasons. The most common response to the inquiry is "Variety is the spice of life!" "Don't get stuck in a rut and allow people around you tell you what to do."

The second most common response falls into the category of "be reasonable."

Here are some of the examples we heard and why the behavior is important to each Grandpa.

"Soup and ham sandwiches are just fine for breakfast. It's not written anywhere we have to eat certain foods for breakfast. It just so happens I enjoy soup and sandwiches. Of course, when there is no soup available, I serve up a plate of cold spaghetti or lasagna. It's mighty fine eating, and I rarely forget dessert."

Another Grandpa said, "I am comfortable in what I wear." It's not unusual to see this octogenarian wearing red or green or blue Converse sneakers with his suit or sports jacket. He said he does it for his grandkids so he can be a hipster. But he adds that it puts him "just off the bubble," and it is a great way of meeting people when they comment on his footwear. Of course, when an important event comes around and he needs to be there, his selection of neckties is not exactly conservative either.

Grooming is very important to certain groups of Grandpas. Some say they shave every day in order to feel better, and "that's just the way it is—men shave!" In the group, there were a few men who commented on personal appearance. Regular haircuts are individual habits for a variety of reasons. Men of their generation are coifed with neat short hairstyles. But there were a couple men who expressed that when it comes to appearance, they choose the "burned-out hippie look." They prefer long hair and beards. Besides taking the guesswork out of their age, they feel it makes a statement to their grandkids that age isn't going to stop them from making those kinds of choices.

A couple Grandpas made statements about the kind of automobiles they drive. One choice involved practicality, while the other involved luxury. "Never pay more than $500 for a car. If you get a fancy newer one and it breaks down, it will cost you more than $500 to get it fixed! Might as well buy another one." There is much truth and wisdom in that thought, if you do not mind driving older cars. His grandkids called his cars "Grandpa's old junkers." Well, it gets him there and back. Others say they prefer a new car because they feel they have earned it in retirement. They claim that a new car will be the last car they ever buy. Some say they buy a new car every three or four years. The reason? They like to drive new cars.

"And if I want to wear my pajamas all day around the house, I will!"

"What's the big deal if I eat garlic every day?"

"If I want to write a letter to some idiot who doesn't have a brain in his head, I will!"

"So I talk to strangers. I think that's interesting!"

"What's the big deal if I stand and wait for the garbageman every week and give him a candy bar?"

"If I want to ride a zip line with my grandkids or dance at the mall, so what?"

Try having your grandkid over for breakfast and serve him chicken wings with ice cream.

Every Grandpa is unique. They all have their own peculiarities. That's what makes them special.

Loss Of A Grandchild

Grandpa, if you have ever experienced the death of a grandchild, it is one of the most gut-wrenching feelings on earth.

The grief is sometimes overwhelming. At first, this thought may go through your mind: *How can I ever recover from this? I loved that kid, and now he is gone. My heart is so full of misery yet overflows with the love and memories of him.*

Hundreds of Grandpas could say they share your feelings, yet nobody really knows what you are going through. And you cannot know for sure what they are experiencing.

So consider this: That baby is safe now. You don't have to be religious or melodramatic to understand this truth. It is a fact that God takes care of babies and young children in eternity. Why? Because first, He loves them. But they do not have a chance to develop a personal relationship with Him. That baby whose life was cut short because of disease or injury or accident did not have the social capacity or mental awareness to make that decision. So the truth is, God loves children and young kids enough to make sure they are in heaven with Him.

That being said, how may Grandpas deal with this loss? Grief is as unique to each individual as snowflakes. There is no formula for grieving and being sad, but neither is there an escape. In some way, everyone must grieve. We cannot look at it as a requirement or a necessity. But in true terms of the process, it is a necessary requirement, and we must deal with it.

Now, we shall never forget. Memories help honor our past and enjoy our future. Certainly, the death of a grandchild is not something you enjoy in the future; however, the joy comes in sharing the fact that you healed from the shock and the sadness. You will always remember that grandkid regardless of the age. The circumstances of his death may help embellish what expectations you had for him, like becoming a scholar or a great musician or a sports star. Do not ever shut the door to the memories. Keep it open and walk through it often.

The separation, at first, may have seemed unbearable. If you knew it was going to happen, even fifty years would not prepare you for it. The road to healing may be a bumpy one. The hole in your heart may be there forever. Life may never be the same, but it still goes on.

We are sorry for your loss. You may have already figured out we cling to our faith tightly. And it is that faith that brings us alongside you and the grief that besets you. It's your memories and your knowledge that God loves you too that will help you realize that as tragic as it may be, everything is going to be all right.

What's On Your Bucket List?

Grandpa, do you have a Bucket List?

A Bucket List is a list of things you want to do before you kick the bucket. It originated long before Jack Nicholson and Morgan Freeman popularized it in a movie by the same name. A famous football coach at a major university told a reporter he kept a list of things he wanted to accomplish that year. He taped it to the door of his office and put a checkmark by the ones that were realized.

"Then," he said, "I keep a secret list in my desk. Those are the things I want to do before I die. It's called 'my Bucket List,' and I'm going to do each one, if I am able, before I kick the bucket!"

Keep a Bucket List. It will do several things for you. It will give you something to look forward to and to work for. It will put anticipation and excitement in your life. A Bucket List will spark your imagination. It will prevent you from being inactive. The list is not a bunch of things that could never happen or things that you do not have an interest in. Things like jumping out of an airplane or wrestling an alligator. Your Bucket List should be doable activities that you may not have considered before. For sure, some of the ideas may stretch you a bit or challenge you. In a sense, that's the whole idea behind having a Bucket List. One Grandpa announced to some of his friends that if he doesn't try new things or travel to other places, he would never know if he could do it. He would always wonder what it might have been like.

Here are some samples of Bucket Lists Grandpas shared with each other at a recent interview session

"I always wanted to drive a NASCAR. I want to go 150 miles per hour on an embanked track and race a dozen other drivers to the finish line." He decided to scratch that item because he learned that drivers are strapped in the cars so tight they could hardly move. They put on a helmet with only a slip for vision. And this Grandpa had claustrophobia, so he erased it from his list. However, he completed some of the items on his list by spitting in the Grand Canyon and the Erie Canal. He performed a stand-up comic routine in front of a legitimate audience and ran a zip line in Las Vegas.

One Grandpa wants to drive an RV across the United States and stop at major college campuses he dreamed of attending as a kid and tour them. The trip would include meeting every president or chancellor of those colleges and universities. He even thought about staying there, living in the RV, and taking a class.

"I want to find a remote cabin in the woods and fish every day for giant salmon. I want to take Grandma and just sit and watch the wild animals."

"My Bucket List includes my grandkids. I want to take all my grandkids on an ocean liner to anywhere. When the ship docks, I want to take side trips with them and eat local foods."

One Grandpa said his Bucket List did not include any activities. He wanted to see everybody in his family be happy and get along with each other. When asked if he thought it was possible, he paused, and with tears in his eyes, said, "I hope so."

What encouragement he received from other Grandpas. They comforted him and shared their journey of trying to accomplish the same thing. And some of them accomplished it. Grandpas report that it can be done.

Another Grandpa wants to perform at Carnegie Hall. He plays the harmonica and whistles (not at the same time). He is quite accomplished in doing both and just dreams of playing and whistling at this famous concert hall.

One of the most unique Bucket List items was a desire to ride a motorcycle, with Grandma on the back, from coast to coast. It's still on the list even though they have considered the dangers of riding a motorcycle at their age. So they decided to buy a convertible and wear helmets!

Some of the Grandpas said they want to meet the president of the United States, toss out the first pitch at the World Series, dress up as the San Diego Chicken and cheer at a Padres baseball game, preach a sermon in the largest church in America, see a Los Angeles Dodgers baseball game, grow orchids and compete at shows, and this is one of the best: "I want a dog that will come to me when I call him and sit on my lap!"

Bucket Lists are fun. You may be surprised. Make your own list and see how dreams can come true.

Sadness

Grandpa, life is not always filled with happy thoughts and happy things. Sometimes it is filled with sadness and tragedy. You don't have any control over those calamities that happen, and they may have a great impact on your life. So what do you do when those times come along?

It would be wonderful if somebody had an answer for you that would erase all the sad times. That is how counselors make a living, and there are some good ones. Pastors are trained for the task of walking people through their sorrow.

Before we look at a few of the circumstances you find yourself in, here is an offer of encouragement. There is a place you can find comfort. There is a place where your questions can be answered without prejudice or judgment.

It's difficult to talk about sensitive things. You never expected your wife to die before you. Sad as you may be, the truth is either the husband or the wife will pass away first. After several decades of marriage, the pain of being referred to as a widower feels strange. Your grief may strike you when the sadness of being left behind is fully realized. Your bride is no longer there to embrace her lover man. Your "girlfriend" may have taught you to cook and do the laundry, but what if she did not. What will you do now? These and a multitude of other things may hit you all at once, and it's hard.

Of course, friends and relatives are there to comfort you with all kinds of clichés that don't really apply. Things like "stay busy" or "time is a great healer." Their intentions are meant well, but the hurt inside you will still be there no matter what you do to make it go away. Grief is so unique to each individual that there is no one fix that fits everyone.

It's just a suggestion, but let's look at what the Bible says about your time of grief. What it says applies to all people whether they are religious or not. It speaks to all people regardless of their faith. The Apostle Peter tells us in his first book (1 Peter 5:10) that God will do something after you have suffered a little while. That is encouraging, but how long is "a little while?" A month? A year? Ten years?

The amount of time will vary with each person. After the suffering, you will be made perfect, strengthened, established, and settled. Let's look at that.

Perfect does not mean you are without flaws or you are suddenly without the warts in your life. It means He will cause you to adjust. Adjustment to life without a partner is possible. He will strengthen you. Like the old blacksmith who got the horseshoes white-hot and dipped them in cold water to strengthen them, you will have a new strength to lift you up so you can carry on. He will also establish you. Here, the word *establish* means "to make firm." How? You have been and will be surrounded by those who love you and care about you. Your demeanor will become firm because you are stronger and are adjusting to life again. And then in this passage, it says He will settle you. The best meaning of this word *settle* is "you are going to be okay." Life will go on, and it will be okay.

We are so sorry for your loss. Sharing with those who have experienced the loss of their partners is a way of expressing our concern for Grandpas.

During this time, don't forget your grandkids. Remember, they lost their grandma. The process of comforting one another can be an experience of growing stronger together.

Grandpa Dating Again

Without a doubt, the feeling may seem weird at first, Grandpa. A major change has taken place in your life, and Grandma is no longer with you. Now you are in a position where you have to decide, "Do I remarry, or do I stay single?"

Well, let's put the pig on the table right from the start. Nobody can make that decision for you. Many will make the attempt, but it is solely your decision. Remember, no decision is a decision. So dealing with the situation will take some courage, some planning, lots of fun, and some research. It's called dating.

Widowers seem to remarry sooner than widows. That is according to statistics. The reason for entering matrimony soon after the death of their spouse is not exactly known because each individual is different and circumstances change. One guess is as good as the other.

The advantage in dating that you have over your grandkids is age and experience. It should be easier for you to do the research, consider the math, and get to work. But it is not always that simple. Feelings and emotions cannot be quantified. In other words, you cannot make a list of planned activities and desires and qualifications, and check off each one, coming to a conclusion like solving a math problem.

There are too many variables. Variables like "Grandma cannot be replaced" and "I was with her for decades, and I cannot forget our life together."

So what do you do? Panic is not one of the options. Take some time and really think about it. Do something besides just sitting all day. Get in the research mode and check out singles groups, churches, and the like. And remember, there are people out there that are in the same boat because their husbands passed away. According to statistics, widows do more research than widowers, so you have the advantage of someone finding you as a lifetime partner.

Certainly, the way you once wooed your sweetheart is different. Chances are, it has not changed all that much, though. Establishing a relationship includes finding something you both enjoy doing, trying new things together, and respecting each other's space. Those elements are timeless, but they take time.

Some of the elements of establishing a relationship in your particular situation can become sensitive. One is working together to decide finances. Cautions include both of you. It may be very important for both of you to know your finances are secure.

Women have a tendency to be more cautious. Depending on how much money they have, they lean toward not getting mixed up with the proverbial parlor snake who is searching for a wealthy widow to scam. But men often watch out for gold diggers who want to improve their standard of living like they never experienced before. Both creatures exist, sad to say.

Another area that is important is affection and sexual understanding. Needless to say, both men and women come from different backgrounds and relationships, and sexual satisfaction can be important. Age is an element as well. Grandpa, when the subject arises, be honest, but don't be shy. One of you will bring it up eventually. Be honest. Both of you are adults.

Finally, dating advice is universal and transcends age. Your grandkids have probably been given dating advice. First step is to join your spirits. Whatever condition your spirit is in, a mismatched spiritual position is a disaster waiting to happen. Then join your minds. This is somewhat flexible but must not be overlooked. Decide the place where you will live, the finances, the joining of a new family, and the acceptance by children and others. Then of course, join your bodies in whatever manner you have discussed. Do not get them out of order.

Concern for Grandpas is our priority. We hope the advice is helpful.

GRANDPA'S LEGACY

Legacy

Grandpa, what will be your legacy? What do you want to leave behind so people will remember you?

The truth of the matter is, if you don't tell somebody or write it down somewhere, chances are, nobody will fulfill your desires. Your legacy will be your gift to friends and family, reminding them how you would like to be remembered. Since it is a gift, maybe it would be better if you chose it instead of allowing somebody else to choose it for you.

Grandpa was thinking about that recently and made it known he did not want his legacy to be that "he was a great skier." He said there were other things in his life he wanted to be known for, and skiing was not one of them. He was kinder than he needed to be and more active than most people in the community. He mowed the lawns of the elderly, delivered food to the hungry, ran errands for the sick, and read the Bible to shut-ins. He received the Community Citizen of the Year Award from the local Chamber of Commerce. People counted on him. In his case, though, his good deeds and exemplary citizenry were overlooked. Everyone just marveled at what a great skier he was. His room was filled with trophies and ribbons, but his heart and spirit were empty.

Grandpas need to communicate with their grand-kids on subjects like legacy. Stroll down a two-way street together and share with each other what kind of legacy you want to leave behind. For a young grandkid, a legacy may seem extremely far in the future. But for a Grandpa, sharing this information could settle an issue within himself and bring light to those around him.

Here is an example. This grandkid wanted to be known for his athletic prowess. He told his Grandpa that when he will die, he wants everyone to wear a baseball cap to his funeral and toss it in the grave. He said he was willing to spend a lifetime building his legacy.

Grandpa could not think of anything to say right away. He sat and was quiet. Then he slowly looked toward the sky and rubbed his chin. "You know, sonny, I guess who you are is more important than what you do. I am really comfortable in my skin. How about you? I have some notable habits and quirks, but that's who I am, not what I am. I love people, and I just want them to be happy. I hope everyone I talk to could know who God is. I like to help people. It gives me a thrill. I love Grandma more than life itself, and she is a gift from Heaven."

His grandson looked at him, and he could see the emotions mounting.

"I never thought of it that way," he said. "That seems to be more important than throwing a baseball. Anyway, what if I break my leg or get hit in the head? And I guess there is an age limit to being a jock."

Grandpa grabbed a long stem of grass and began to chew on it. It was quiet even longer than the last time.

"Look, your legacy is your own. It's not something you hear another person say and then try to adopt something like it as your own. I just think it's something we all should give serious thought to."

Shortly after their conversation, Grandpa had a stroke and couldn't speak. He and his grandson continued to communicate well. Their eye contact connected their spirits, and holding hands didn't hurt either. It was as though they were having a conversation and understood what the other person was feeling. Quite often, after his Grandpa passed away, the grandson gave some serious thought to the legacy talk. It made him a better person.

Grandpa, You Are Being Watched!

What a surprise it was when Grandpa came to the realization that his grandkids paid more attention to his words and actions than he had ever imagined. He was teaching them, whether he realized it or not.

Let's take a look at some of the things we heard at a recent Grandkids' Town Hall meeting. The following are unedited responses to the question "What did you learn from your Grandpa?"

- "Always leave things better than when you found them."
- "I've learned the importance of faith, discipline, and love from my Grandpa."
- "I learned to cook eggs."
- "How to eat candy!"
- "I learned resourcefulness to survive on very little. He and Grandma modeled prayer and peace."
- "The bigger they are, the harder they fall!"
- "How to use a leaf blower and play golf."
- "Don't be afraid to look stupid once in a while!"
- "Never give up." (He had cancer for nine years)
- "My Grandpa taught me to identify car brands. We went to some amazing car shows."
- "I learned to enjoy life more by appreciating family and small things."
- "Why be difficult when you can be impossible!"

Countless young people and adults shared how their Grandpas taught them what the value of hard work was and how to work hard. Several testimonies were given regarding working smart. The love for Grandpa that permeated the room was amazing. A few grandkids noted that they had a very strong desire to know more about their Grandpas, but their Grandpas never told them anything of significance until they asked him. Then the floodgates opened. There were stories of Grandpa playing professional baseball, working as a spy, coming to America with literally nothing, and building a very successful business. Some of the grandkids learned how their Grandpas did some wild and crazy things when they were young. A couple then said, "I had no idea Grandpa was so normal and did some of the most unbelievable things."

The story was told that one Grandpa, when he was very young, was raised in an era when the teacher or principal could use a paddle as a form of punishment. He called it the "board of education." Grandpa was called out for sassing the teacher and had an appointment with the principal, but he never showed up. The teacher and several faculty members went looking for him and found him on the roof of the school. Grandpa refused to come down, and they called the fire department to retrieve him. Of course, his mom and dad were embarrassed. Grandpa escaped the paddle but was expelled from school. That probably hurt more than the spanking.

Grandpa, do not underestimate your wisdom, humor, and ability to be a role model. Believe it or not, your grandkids are watching your actions and listening to your every word.

Setting Up A Foundation

Grandpa and Grandma told us they wanted to help us get an education.

Education is getting more and more expensive. College has advanced from "a great option" to "a necessity." The technology in all lines of work has made formal education or training a requirement for employment.

Grandpa said, "Here's the deal. We can't pay for everything, but we can help. We have set up a foundation for all our grandkids, and they can draw on it to help go to college or trade school or technical school."

The foundation is under the IRS Tax Code as 529. It is a tax-deductible contribution that anyone can make. It is used for the purpose of education. The originators of the fund have control over it and manage it. When money is withdrawn for education, it is not taxed. If money is withdrawn for something else, it is taxed.

Grandpa told us they set it up when we were babies, and it has increased in size due to compound interest. Aunts and uncles and other friends and relatives have increased the size of it with their contributions. Grandma and Grandpa have faithfully contributed a fixed amount every year.

So if one of us grandkids wants to be a shoemaker or a chef or a doctor or an accountant, they are behind us all the way.

In true Grandpa fashion, here comes a story. "I remember when I worked my way through school. I had three jobs. Back then, minimum wage was $1.10 an hour. Gas was twenty-six cents a gallon, and you could buy a new car for under a thousand dollars. But school wasn't cheap even back then."

He went on to tell us tuition was eighty-eight dollars a quarter, and if you spent more than thirty-five dollars on books, you paid too much. But with most colleges and universities today reaching $40,000 or $50,000 a year, we all need help.

This is a great way for our whole family to get help with our educations, thanks to Grandpa and Grandma.

Dr. and Mrs. McKinley have seen two grandchildren graduate from major universities debt-free as a result of the Foundation. Both grandparents and their grandkids are blessed with a wonderful relationship.

ABOUT THE AUTHORS

Dr. David Sutton was raised in a military family and traveled and lived in several states and foreign countries. He has a BA in journalism from Eastern Washington State College (now EWU) and has worked for several newspapers as a feature writer and general reporter. He has authored several magazine articles as a freelance writer. After serving as a military journalist in the US Army, Dr. Sutton began studying for ministry at Southwestern Baptist Theological Seminary. He holds a Doctorate in Conflict Management from Trinity Theological Seminary. He and his wife, Vickie, have four grown children and fifteen grandkids. They reside in Spokane, Washington.

Dr. Blake McKinley grew up in Alaska and holds a BEd from the University of Alaska. After teaching mathematics in Alaska schools for a short time, he graduated from the University of Missouri, Kansas City Dental School; and Boston University School of Dentistry. He has practiced dentistry in Kodiak, Alaska, and endodontics in Spokane, Washington. And he is now retired. He and his wife, Joan, have four grown children and twelve grandkids. They reside in Spokane, Washington, where Dr. McKinley is active in his church. He has taken several missionary trips to many foreign countries where he served as a dentist on the medical team.

The Grandpa's Manual is the first book for both writers.